BIG LOVE, 29655-057

Big Love
29655-057
Posts from Prison

DAVID JOSEPH GARIANO

OUR INSIDE VOICES PUBLISHING

CONTENTS

FOREWORD

The incarcerated. Unless you know one of them, you can forget they exist. Meet Dave Gariano 29655-057, sentenced to five years in federal prison for growing marijuana.

Here are a few things you won't forget after meeting Dave. Lights are never out and the only respite from the clamor and din of prison life is in the morning's wee hours when the other 129 men in your bunkroom are snoring, mostly oblivious to the frequent flushing of toilets and jingling keys of the guards doing their every two-hour census count. How to make "ice cream" from milk and grape jelly in a small garbage can, that chess is a big deal in prison, and it is absolutely possible to bank shot love and longing off a full moon directly to your sleeping BabyO 300 miles away. Also, in the day-in-and-out monotony of prison life, when counting the days, weeks, months, years to when you'll get out, "staying in the here and now is critical for doing time well."

Big Love is a big-hearted love letter and metaphysical meander within and without two West Virginia federal prison camps. Seated at a "tiny grey steel table, writing before the sun comes up, by the glare of the sodium perimeter lights" the author transports us from the confines of prison to his inner-city, "post-apocalyptic" Pittsburgh boyhood to an environmentally eye-opening stint on a Louisiana shrimp trawler, to his six-month revelatory refuge in a redwood forest in northern California (sleeping on rainy nights in the hollow 20-foot diameter, 15-foot high stump of a logged ancient Sequoia). Vignettes of a former freewheeling life intertwine seamlessly with the sensory overload-deprivation of many men living cheek-to-jowl behind bars.

The similar sad fate of a flamed-headed, freckled boy and a fluorescent-yellow dime store Easter peep; the "taints and bruises" of the ubiquitous "purplish rubbery meat composite, Turkey Ham";

the caged-monkey mentality of lockdown; the prolonged, mindful invocation of aesthetic pleasure siphoned from the selection, drying, and arranging of tiny wildflowers found along an asphalt walking track. Bounded in a place and situation most unnatural, the author grasps the lifeline of any and all connection with the natural world and human condition in order to do his time "well," that is, sanely and creatively, undergirded with a keen sense of absurdist humor.

Dave 29655-057 is a very real person, "a man like any man." And, more than anything, he wants us to understand that the incarcerated are not solely defined by prison. "I'm not a convict who took almost six decades to come to prison," he writes. "I've been a son, a father, a husband, a hippy, a professional, a neighbor, and a friend. ...All these experiences culminate in shaping and defining who I am. Now I add to these elements the experience of being arrested, prosecuted, and incarcerated."

Dave tells his own and other inmates' stories, to "put a human face on people caught up in a dehumanizing system." The reader will not forget his highly original voice or Georgie, Black Kitchen Frank, or Omer and the thousand oranges.

Here's something else that ought not to be forgotten and *must cease*: All the life, love, and talent that has been lost in this county's failed war on drugs. Most specifically, the irrevocable damage perpetrated against hundreds of thousands of marijuana users and growers.

So pull up a metal chair alongside Dave Gariano, 29655-057. Bear witness to a big thinker and gifted raconteur enmeshed within America's gargantuan, for-profit prison system. The "land of the free" that incarcerates more of its citizens than any other country in the world—the vast majority being non-violent drug offenders.

Constance Bumgarner Gee

Author of *Higher Education: Marijuana at the Mansion*

PREFACE

I t's 7:30 on a Sunday morning at Beckley Federal Prison Camp in mid-October of 2016. I've been wanting to put together an introduction to this collection of my writing, much of it done in the early morning hours at this prison, and the last joint I was in.

I've already been up for hours, done pill line, ate breakfast, and walked a couple of laps around the rec yard. My wife, Diane, told me, and sent some supporting articles, that walking will help my writing. As with so many things, she is right.

Last night I was working on a different draft of this same paper in the prison library but shortly after I started we had an inclement weather count. Rain bands spinning off Hurricane Matthew in North Carolina stretched all the way to where I am on top of Sandstone Mountain in West Virginia. It brought wind and rain and fog. We often get fog here and when we do we get a census count, too. The guards call everyone back to our cells/cubes and do a headcount. It's a typical prison experience to be arbitrarily interrupted and I've learned to live with it in the past two years I've been incarcerated. The whole prison experience interrupts our lives, our families, our communities, our hopes and dreams and aspirations in a profound way.

As inmates, these interruptions are part of a bigger prison experience that shapes and influences us. However, by themselves, they don't define us. That's what I hope my writing informs the reader of. I'm not a convict who took almost six decades to come to prison. I'm a man like any man.

My life has been full and varied. I've been a son, a father, a husband, a hippy, a professional, a neighbor, and a friend. I spent 29 years in the insurance industry and I spent five years hitch hiking around North America living out of a bag and a bedroll. All of these experiences culminate in shaping and defining who I am. Now I add to these elements the experience of being arrested, prosecuted, and incarcerated. These are components of who I am just like all the experiences in my life are.

If there is one point I want my writing to bring to light, it's that every man I've known in prison is a real person. They are not simply or fully defined by their imprisonment. I've tried to put a human face on people caught up in a dehumanizing system. I've tried to do this by telling parts of their story and bits and pieces of mine. They are stories too big to be contained by prison walls, and way too big to be defined by what I can write.

This book consists of a series of posts to my Facebook account that I wrote after beginning my incarceration. I don't have internet access so I'd email them to Diane and she'd post them for me and send me the comments. It was and still is a great way for me to stay connected to my extended family and friends and I'm very fortunate that Diane has facilitated this for me.

Now I hope they can reach a bigger audience. I hope too, that in reading this epistolary that every reader comes to realize that the human tragedy caused by the trend of mass incarceration sweeping our country for the past several decades isn't just a hypothetical construct of social scientists and bleeding heart leftists. It's a tragedy that engulfs the lives of millions of Americans, one human being at a time.

I hope my writing touches you, the reader, and moves you to action. My deepest desire is that Americans, once informed of the human consequences of our national policies, will rise to the challenge and change those policies that now only focus on fear and punishment for profit. I hope we will, instead, institutionalize compassionate, intelligent, and constructive laws that will enhance the lives of every citizen.

Big Love,
Dave 29655-057

GREETINGS FROM GILMER FEDERAL PRISON

NOVEMBER, 2014

I 'm writing this as an inmate from Gilmer Federal Prison in Glenville, WV. I don't have access to the internet but I'm sending this to Diane and she's agreed to post it to my page. I won't be able to see any comments, but you can put something on there if you want to share it with others who read it. I'll also post my address at the end in case you'd like to write to me directly. Please bear in mind all mail is read by prison officials before I see it. They have zero sense of humor or irony. Photos are allowed.

How I got here. In early December of 2012 police raided our home in Burlington, NC and arrested Diane and me for growing marijuana. They seized a car, and cash on hand, and other property, in addition to the marijuana and for a year we faced state charges while our attorney worked through the legal system. In December 2013 we were rearrested for the same crime by federal authorities and the state charges were dropped. Eventually by March, 2014 we accepted a plea bargain that included three years of probation (including 6 months of house arrest) for Diane and five years of prison for me based on mandatory minimum sentencing rules. Sentencing was in June of 2014. Diane's probation began immediately and my self reporting was delayed until October 17, 2014 to accommodate the surgeries I had scheduled for my hip, pelvis, and knee. As of this Friday November 14 I will have been incarcerated for one month. I will write additional posts on our arrest and prosecution, my appeal process, as well as my experience in prison. I hope to lend insight into life here, my fellow inmates, the penal system, and the effects of incarceration on the individual, family, friends, business, and society, from my vantage point.

The purpose of this first post is to make our family and friends aware of our circumstance. I also want to make people aware that in this age where half the people in the United States live in states where marijuana has been legalized for medicinal and or recreational use, the Federal Government continues to prosecute and imprison 10's of thousands of non-violent marijuana users and growers. Last year the fed spent $41 billion on it's war on marijuana and sent thousands to prison for 5-40 years under mandatory minimum sentencing guidelines. In a time when most Americans think the government is becoming more enlightened, the reality is the exact opposite. The state and federal prisons are bursting at the seams with more than 2 1/2 million prisoners, more than half with nonviolent drug crimes. In the last decade prison populations have increased 400%. In addition tens of millions family members and business associates suffer hardships caused by this insane trend of accelerated incarcerations. Society as a whole is decreased by the practice which could be at best described as a modern day slave trade for profit.

Here I am at my tiny grey steel table, writing before the sun comes up, by the glare of the sodium perimeter lights, shining in through my window. I know what you'll think when you read this. I start so many stories like this. It's repetitious. Believe me, I know. One aspect of prison life is the sameness of each day. It's an important reason to focus on today while doing time. Otherwise you'll only torture yourself. Staying in the here and now is critical to doing time well. That goes for me in here where I am and, I bet, for you wherever you are, too. If you let the shit stack up, it'll wig you out.

So I start writing by noting where I am and trying to be in the present. Once I establish this in my mind and fix it through my pencil on paper, I can use it as a point of departure. It's one of those quirky dichotomies we have to live with. I've been unlearning my conventional beliefs of time and space but in doing so I've also got to recognize how useful they are as a frame of reference. As I accept the basic premise of who, and where, and when I am, it becomes easier for me to leave it behind. What springs to mind is train travel. Before I go anywhere I have to start by being at the station at a fixed time. After that point the analogy fails. Buying a train ticket one has a destination in mind.

PART 1. PITTSBURGH

We're thinking of getting our place in Friar's Hill logged. We've had that place for almost 40 years. Initially, we cleared an acre or so for our house and garden. Diane and I cut the trees, dug the stumps by hand, and burned the brush piles, making a place for ourselves to live and raise our babies. In turn, that clearing has been a beautiful woodland meadow for the last 30 years. Since then, most years, I've cut several loads of firewood for our house and for our friends. By and large the remaining 21 acres of mixed hardwoods have been growing unimpeded. During that time I've introduced five or six species of saprophytic mushrooms to help replenish the carbon load that has been diminished in the soil from previous generations of logging. We haven't had livestock there and that has promoted a healthy understory and tremendous biodiversity.

During the last 40 years I've calculated, on a number of occasions, the carbon sequestration capacity of this woodlot and it easily exceeds the carbon footprint of my driving and heating my home during that same time. By comparison, someone who drives or flies or heats a home without maintaining a wood lot is ignoring a basic tenant of sustainability, which is to do as little harm as possible and be responsible for the pollution they do make.

The more someone drives or flies, the bigger the house one heats and cools, or the colder/hotter climate one lives in, then the more pollution that person generates, as a matter of course. Ideally such a person would maintain a larger woodlot, or in some other capacity accommodate for their consumptive habits. Someone in a cold environment with a lawn and few if any trees and who travels regularly is likely generating a disproportionately large environmental imbalance on an individual scale when it comes to carbon footprints. Home heating with oil or coal or electricity adds significantly to the problem.

If the shoe fits, wear it, or alternately, use it to beat your friends and act like your not the problem. It is a point of some solace to me over the last 40 years to see that the regenerative aspect of appropriate small plot woodland management is viable and how the greenhouse gas generation and sequestration circle can be completed by anyone who cares enough to act on it. It's easy to imagine a direct correlation with the carbon gasses we've created and the carbon gasses sequestered by the trees on our place.

Diane and our boys and I once lived on that place in a tiny 300 square foot cabin we built in 1980 and that still stands. Diane gave birth to our youngest son, Yuri, in that cabin. The cabin is eight locust posts set in the ground with stringers nailed to them and siding of 5 quarter, rough cut lumber from a small local saw mill. One of these posts is actually a living locust tree I lobbed off at about 10 feet and used in situ. It lived on and has sprouted new branches each year, often into the bedroom. When I last saw the cabin two and a half years ago that tree was still growing.

The entire cabin sits directly under a large locust tree perhaps 50 feet tall and two feet in diameter, in a much larger grove of mixed hardwoods. White oak, red oak, some hickories, and a few big chokecherries. Dogwood and redbud crouch throughout the understory. The big locust is very cool, mostly dead, and the home to a great colony of big black carpenter ants.

There had been a second locust tree of similar size about 10 feet away but it died years ago and I bucked it up. We burned the twisted thorny branches in campfires, the ashes melting back into the soil from which they came. Half a dozen of the bigger rounds we kept for camp stools and the rest of it ended up as stove wood for friends in Lewisburg, or as fireplace wood at our house, where the ashes helped feed our garden.

One more story about the two big locust trees. More than 35 years ago, when we were living beneath their canopy, there was a tremendous locust bloom with hundreds if not thousands of flowering clusters covering both trees. Locust blooms look like wisteria except on these trees they were pure white. Oh, the smell! Wonderful and sweet beyond measure, our yard was thick with the aroma of the locust trees' sexual desire. More potent than lilac, the only tree I've ever known to match the saccharine intensity of locust were the Jacaranda trees at dusk in South Africa.

I had a strong hive of bees in the garden that year, two deep hive bodies worth, maybe 30 or 40,000 workers, filling their hive and 3 supers with clear, sweet, fragrant locust honey. At night the hive sounded like an idling diesel truck engine from the activity of the worker bees standing over each cell in the honeycomb, fanning it with their wings to evaporate the water out of the honey before sealing it closed. After dark Diane and I, each with a baby, would go up to the garden to feel the resonance of the bees working their alchemy and to soak in the aroma of the honey. In my memory, my wife, my babies, my bees, my trees, my land, my night. I owned them all, as surely as they owned me.

Sitting now in prison at my tiny writing table, I own that time and place and everything in it. I am rich.

APRIL, 2016

Mid-April and every day the sun rises a little farther to the north. The window in my cell has a northern exposure and throughout the winter there wasn't a time when I had a direct view of the sun. All that changed about a week ago. The tilting of the earth on its axis has progressed to the point where I now get some direct sunbeams at dawn and for a short while afterwards. The trees in my field of view have yet to leaf out. The branches, the buds, and the moment seem pregnant with it. When the leaves come out they'll obscure my view of the rising sun, but I should still get some direct rays as the sun lifts above the canopy. I don't begrudge the trees the sunbeams, they must be hungry after their long winter's fast.

Directly in front of my window, perhaps 40 yards distant, in a small grove of young white oaks, one of the first heralds of spring is the blooming of a serviceberry tree, or sarvis as they are commonly referred to. The sparse white flowers stayed on during our last snow and continue flowering still.

Thirty-five years ago I heard a poem about a sarvis in bloom written by a midwife who found herself walking through deep spring snow in the mountains of West Virginia, to a remote location, to assist with a birth. The difficulty of the trek, the steep terrain, the impediment of the drifting snow all stacked against her, taxing her resolve until she reached a point where she considered turning back. Just at that time she came upon a sarvis tree in bloom. Small compared to other trees, spare in bloom, convoluted in conformity, she saw the tree's frail tenacity and was inspired to walk on, eventually arriving in time to assist with the childbirth and the arrival of a new member of the forest community.

I don't recall the name of the woman who wrote the poem. I heard her recite it on our little battery powered radio, in our tiny cabin, not long after Diane gave birth to our second baby boy. From that poem, what has stuck with me through the years is the sense of community between trees and people, the vivacious and heroic nature of both the sarvis tree and the midwife, and the beauty and strength of resolution all life is possessed of in striving for procreation.

There is something too, to be said of the lingering power of poets and poetry. All of this comes to me now seeing the little sarvis tree blooming in the grove of oaks outside my prison window. That was not the story I wanted to tell. My pencil was hijacked by the spirit of the sarvis. The story I want to tell is about a stump thousands of years old and thousands of miles from here.

I grew up in Pittsburgh during the 1950s and 60s. I started high school the year Dr. Martin Luther King was assassinated and the year I graduated was the the same year the draft ended for the Vietnam War. The rioting of the civil rights movement was happening where I lived and I was part of it. For years the neighborhood I was raised in was embroiled in violence and animosity. As a teenager I was dying to get out of there. My best friend Pete and I made plans to escape all though our senior year of high school. We both worked and saved our money. On our days off we'd walk the streets and strategize our exit.

Ten days after graduating high school, on the morning of my 18th birthday I left home with Pete. It was June of 1973. We both had backpacks, a few changes of clothes, a bedroll, and a couple of bucks in our pockets. We hitchhiked through New England, sleeping on roadsides, in culverts, under overpasses, or camped in parks. We slept almost anywhere we found ourselves at nightfall. Much of that summer we lived at Mount Batty State Park outside Camden, Maine. I worked as a breakfast grill cook at a nearby diner on US 1.

Done with that we traveled north through Quebec Province. As fall arrived, we thumbed back to Pittsburgh to check in with our families then back on the road again. Autumn's chill drove us to Galveston, Texas.

I spent the fall and winter and following spring working on shrimp trawlers, plying the Gulf coast from Louisiana to Mexico. We fished the beaches and the deep water, each in their season. Pete got a room in a boarding house and worked the day labor pool at the port unloading cargo ships euphemistically called banana boats. I'd be on the water 12-15 days at a time then spend the few days ashore at Pete's place sleeping on the floor and cursing the Palmetto bugs.

Come late spring we hitched north again, getting robbed at gunpoint outside Houston, then working together for six weeks delivering furniture in Wichita Falls, Oklahoma. Eventually we made our way back to Pittsburgh. Pete had grown tired of travel and decided to stay. I was back on the road, this time alone. Back in Texas in a couple weeks, back on shrimp boats in a few days, working a variety of trawlers until the following spring. I left the boats to hitchhike to Mardi Gras. Mardi Gras was nothing like I expected. I was expecting fun but found only debauchery. Spending about ten days in New Orleans I left following my thumb to the San Francisco Bay Area, Berkeley in specific. It was my first transcontinental trip.

In Berkeley I connected with a friend from Pittsburgh, Robbie G. who introduced me to another friend of his named Ed. Ed was a publisher and owned a tract of land about 100 miles north of the Bay Area in Sonoma County. He was looking for someone to live there and do some chores in exchange for a few groceries every other week when he would come to visit. He had 55 acres that had been subdivided on paper only from a 7,000 acre tract. It was all rolling hills rising 1,000 feet above the Pacific Ocean and covered in Redwoods, meadows, steep canyons hollowed by cascading creeks, and panoramic views of the forest and the water.

Fronted on one side by California Highway 101, the Pacific Coastal Highway (PCH), it lay about five miles north of Jenner-by-the-Sea. At that time Jenner was a tiny hamlet. A few houses and a post office inside the general store, with a front porch that overlooked the Russian River spilling into the sea. The river had pushed a great bar of rubble and rock into the ocean, building a peninsular jetty--a favorite basking spot for seals and sea lions. Driving north the gate to the ranch, so called because a couple thousand sheep were turned out to graze the ridge top meadows, was on the right. To the left was a small rocky cove favored by Abalone divers and people who would build temporary beach houses from the copious amounts of driftwood.

The ranch was entered through a steel gate and from there a gravel and dirt road wound serpentine up into the hills. It followed the ridge tops several miles inland, weaving along the high ground of what is called the coastal range. It was soft in wet weather and dusty in dry weather. It climbed through spectacular redwood forests, logged a hundred years or more prior. After the old growth trees had been cut each stump sprouted a ring of secondary growth trees. Each of these trees had grown 60-100 feet tall and 2-4 feet in diameter in the passing of a century or more.

The original old growth trees were 15-30 feet in diameter and the new generation sported a skirt of branches all the way to the ground so that each of these enormous "fairy rings" could easily be 100 feet across. The low branches obscured the stumps inside each circle. Driving by or even standing nearby each of these groves appeared as a random cluster hiding the true nature of these congregations of sentinels.

Maybe 3 miles inland a side road followed a sharp cutback to the right to a secondary gate.

Through the gate and down a steep draw, the road was notched into the side of the ridge like an ant trail beneath the giant trees. It led to an outcropping, a level clearing of several acres with a western exposure and an expansive view. Perhaps 800 feet above sea level the vista fell precipitously down a steeply wooded canyon, cut from the hills by a stream that tumbled through boulders and fallen redwoods lying in complex logjams the length of the valley. The clearing was a turn at the head of the canyon closing off one end, while the other end of the canyon opened to the cove where we had entered the first gate, and to the greater ocean beyond. During the days traffic on the PCH could be faintly heard as trucks down shifted through the descents and curves and labored their engines on the climbs. At quiet times when the wind blew onto land it carried the sound of the surf with it.

Around the edges of the clearing were some bay trees and pin oaks and following the curve of the outcropping the woods reverted to redwood forest. On the lip of the canyon was one of the circular groves hiding a massive stump 15 feet tall and 25 feet across. It had been cut high because of a hollow center. A head high cleft in the base permitted a person to stoop and turn sideways to enter a conical void shaped much like the interior of a teepee. 15 feet wide on the floor it narrowed to a hole a foot across at the top and slightly off center. The floor was spongy and soft with a thousand years of heartwood duff.

I would stay on this property for the next nine months. Many nights I would sleep under the stars with a fire for company. About an equal number of nights I would sleep in the cavity of the stump. I would call this tree my home. Living in this big woods of big trees for most of my 20th year, I would change forever who I was, more than I could have ever imagined in those first few days. I would become as wild and free as was possible in modern America. and at night I would be cradled in the literal heart of a giant. This is the story I want to tell.

Again I am seated at my tiny gray steel writing table, in my plastic chair. looking out the window. This morning the fog is so thick I can only make out a very few of the closest trees. We have been called back to our housing units and cells for a "fog count" and the rec yard has been cleared. The fog is dense and the air is still. Nothing moves. When I lived in Greenbrier County, an hour to the east of here, we would get a lot of fog, especially in the summer. It would settle in the valleys and creek beds, like a thinner, less viscous version of those waterways. Here on Sandstone Mountain the fog has the qualities of a cloud snagged on a rock premonitory.

When I lived in Sonoma County California, along the coast, the summer fog would form over the ocean and migrate on to the land. By midday it would burn off into the sky. A sort of reverse rainfall as the ocean changed to vapor, climbed up the valleys, over the hills, then rose into the sky. Off the coast the submerged forests of Giant Pacific Kelp depend on a upwelling of nutrient laden currents from the deep and likewise, the coastal redwood forests depend for much of the year on an upwelling of fog from the ocean. In fact the redwoods only grow as far inland as the fog penetrates. I read once that a large redwood tree might condense and assimilate as much as 2,000 gallons of water a day from the fog. More than seven tons of water per day, only to be off gassed later the same day in the heat of the sun. Assimilation and transpiration. A great breathing of water.

I have a window in my cell. I really like it. It looks out onto a grassy area for about 50 feet, then across a gravel perimeter road and from there the ground falls away into a steep sided wooded hollow. The trees are mostly deciduous hardwoods, particularly white oaks that are easy to spot because they are still holding on to last year's leaves. All the trees are young, the biggest a foot in diameter and 40 feet tall. Most are much smaller. Virtually all of them have multiple trunks growing from the stumps of the last generation of trees. By all appearances the entire landscape must have been clear cut just prior to building this prison.

Just to the right of center in my view is a very tall steel pole, maybe 75 feet tall, with an array of high intensity discharge sodium lights on top. Six powerful lamps arraigned like the petals of a daisy and always lit at night. This morning when I started to write this it was still a couple of hours before dawn, and the light shining through my window was bright enough to write by. It's like a super night light and while it's not very conducive to sleep, it's great for reading and writing at night after "lights out" is in effect.

I do love having a window in my cell and being able to see the trees. I so admire their stoicism. I don't anthropomorphize them at all. It would be such a disservice to them. They are bigger and longer lived than us and as a group almost 1,000 times as numerous as people. I read a recent estimate, derived by NOAA from satellite photos ,that there are still about four trillion trees alive right now on Earth. In spite of the constant war of attrition waged on trees by people, termites, insects, fungi, bacterium, disease, *ad infinitum*, they thrive. They get by eating sunlight, drinking rain, and are apparently happy to stay in one place their entire life. They live in perfect symbiosis with thousands of other species.

They give us the air we breath, provide shelter and food, clean the water, moderate the temperature of the planet, and perform a myriad of other functions beneficial to us and all the Earth's biosphere. They do it without pay or reward and without bitching or moaning. They do all this even as we exercise our relentless forces of annihilation on them. They are sunlight manifest and we turn them into toilet paper as quickly as we can. So no, I won't dishonor them with personification. We should strive for such stoic nobility.

I *wrote the preceding on Sunday morning. It is now 8 am Monday morning. I sit in the same plastic chair, at the same tiny steel writing table, in front of the same window. The same trees stand before me, unmoved since yesterday. I'm waiting for census count to be called. It is a standing count, meaning guards will walk through our housing unit and we, the inmates, will be standing quietly in our cells. As the guards walk by with a clipboard and pen we will each recite our name and number, to be checked off the list.*

13

We do this several times a day. Early morning, early afternoon, 4 PM, and 10 PM. We are also counted at midnight, 3 AM and 5AM, but we don't need to stand for those counts.

While I wait I watch the trees. They are animated and stirred by the wind.

I know that this time of year when the trees are just starting to flower and form leaf buds, but not yet leafed out, that the stirring by the wind accelerates the capillary action in the cambium cells of the trees, facilitating the pumping of large quantities of sap containing water and minerals and sugars from deep in the ground to the tree's highest extremities. When we used to make Maple syrup, we would take advantage of this action. Trees would bleed most profusely at the taps during windy periods with freezing nights and thawing days. Each tree pumping thousands of pounds of water and nutrients in preparation for blooming and leafing out.

This passive system of moving bodily fluids seems in many ways superior to the mechanical heart pumps of animals which so often fail us. Perhaps this explains the stoicism of trees. They have no heart to break. Maybe in Nature's headlong rush into evolution, the driving tendency toward complexity has imbued us with an Achilles' heel in the form of our heart.

JUNE, 2016

I just got back to my housing unit after breakfast. I've found a relatively quiet place to write this morning in "the bubble". It's a room about 20 by 15 feet in one of our housing units that until a few weeks ago housed eight men. Eight bunks, eight lockers, four tiny writing tables, four table lamps, and eight adult men. It also has two large, heavy, plate glass windows to the central hallway and two smaller stationery exterior windows.

When eight guys lived in this room it was crowded, loud, and stinky. Now the room has been emptied and inmates have stripped the floor and washed the walls.

They've set up two folding tables and when the guards unlock the door we are allowed to use it as a study hall.

As I said it's relatively quiet for prison, although the wall I'm facing separates the bubble from the bathroom. Its the wall where the urinals are mounted and the sound of flushing is almost continuous. Still, the only voices I can hear are muted, and the room doesn't smell bad, and there are two windows. like that. I used to live in a cell with a window but my cell assignment was changed a few weeks ago and I was moved to a cell in the interior of the building. Cells are reassigned on an irregular basis and I was lucky to have the last one for 10 months, with a window and a view of the woods.

Where I'm sitting now has a view that's nice too. Right outside are some white oaks and one red oak, then the volleyball court, and beyond that more trees and the ground falls away. On the oaks right outside the window, two pairs of woodpeckers are dashing back and forth, occasionally stopping to pound their faces into the trees. They seem to be doing more flitting about than eating. Perhaps they are just enjoying the morning air. One pair is about the size of starlings and a dull gray color, very similar in tone to the bark of the white oaks. The other pair are roughly the size of finches, mostly gray but with distinct black and white about the head. It's nice to sit by the window undisturbed and enjoy their company while I write.

Next weekend is Father's Day and so I've been thinking a lot about my Dad. He's been dead for almost 30 years now. He was a good man. No saint to be sure, but then no one is. I only knew him for the second half of his life.

While I was growing up he was a mail carrier in Pittsburgh. He had that job for 25 years or so and retired from the post office. Most of that time he delivered mail in the same black neighborhood, right next to where I grew up. When the post office unionized he took on the responsibility of becoming the shop steward for his branch. It was so like him to do that.

He enjoyed being an active integer in the social organizations he was a part of. At the small Lutheran church I was raised in he was always on church council, sometimes president of the congregation, head of the evangelism committee, and he started and edited the church newsletter "the Trumpeteer".

As a boy I always liked to help him run off copies on a hand crank mimeograph machine with its potent chemical odors. Each crank of the handle rotated the print drum and turned out another page. The stencils he typed out on his ancient Underwood typewriter had to be inked by hand and wrinkled easily. He and I, together in the basement office, beneath the Parrish Hall, cranking out page after page. chunka, chunka, chunka, chunka. We collated them by hand, stapled the pages together and stuck address labels on each one. To this day I interchange the word mimeograph for printing or copying, though I haven't seen one of those machines in 45 years.

My Dad would organize a big picnic for the church congregation each year at Riverview Park, a city park about a mile from our church, and another picnic for the postal workers, and their families, from the post office where he worked. Both picnics were similar and lots of fun with softball, and games organized by age group. Most games had prizes for the winners. There were three-legged sack races and races carrying a raw egg on a spoon held in one's mouth. For little kids there were peanut scrambles. My Dad would buy a big burlap sack of peanuts roasted in the shell and mix in a handful of nickels and a couple pounds of Clark Peanut Butter Kisses. Damn, I loved those candies, I wonder if they still make them.

One peanut would have a colored string tied around it. Some adults would toss handfuls of the peanut, coin, and candy mix out into the grass and all the little kids would scramble to collect them. Of course the peanut with the colored string won a prize. There were games for the adults too. One of my favorites was when they'd form two big lines facing each other and starting only a couple feet apart, each pair was given a water balloon. They'd toss them back and forth and on each successful catch the lines would take a step backwards, increasing the distance of each subsequent throw. It was great fun to see the adults soak themselves as the balloons burst. The last balloon intact won a prize for the couple who held it.

Both picnics had washtubs filled with ice water and floating 7 oz. pony bottles of Regent brand sodas. The mailmen had ice cold Iron City beer from kegs. One of the best parts about hanging out with my Dad was going around to get supplies for the picnics. We'd go to Jewish wholesalers near Penn Avenue in the strip district to buy a big sack of peanuts and toy prizes, the Clark Candy company to get the candy kisses. One of my favorite stops was on the morning of the picnic. My Dad and I would go to the ice house that was located on his mail route.

The place was run and staffed by powerfully built black men wielding needle sharp, pointed, scissoring, ice tongs. They used to throw around 50 lb blocks of ice like Legos, and they all knew I was Joe Gariano's boy. I can remember going there in the summer sometimes to see my Dad when he was working his route, and they would stand a big block of ice on end on the battered wooden loading dock, covering it with a burlap sack for me to sit on while I visited.

All these guys liked my Dad and that seemed to be the case anywhere I went with him. He was self confident and gregarious, a salt of the earth, blue collar man. People respected him. He was stocky built with powerful arms and legs and a barrel chest along with broad, muscled hands. I remember being very young and wrestling with just one of his hands while he watched TV, apparently unaware that I was putting my all into prying open just one finger. Just when I was sure his fingers would never unclench from a fist, he would flash open his hand and before I could seize the opportunity it would close again.

I remember one time when I was about 8 and my mother was dying from cancer, she was scheduled for an operation that would require a significant transfusion of blood. At the time Red Cross would allow a 2 for 1 credit if friends would donate blood. I don't know how much she required but when my father announced the blood drive at work more than 30 people showed up and gave. Most had never met my mother but they donated because they knew my Dad.

My Dad's workday started early, 6 AM, and he was done by 2:30 in the afternoon. Some days when I wasn't in school, on a Saturday or in the summer, I would walk the couple of miles from our house to the Post office where he worked. The post office at that time was a beautiful stone building that is now a Carnegie Public Library next door to the Buhl Planetarium. I'd enter through the loading docks at the rear of the building through double swinging steel doors with "DO NOT ENTER" stenciled on them and a million tiny dings from being rammed by the wheeled carts used to transfer mail sacks between trucks and the sorting floor. The sorting floor consisted of a couple hundreds of standing desks, each one in front of a wide bay of pigeon holes, each pigeon hole representing an address on the carrier's route. Each work station had a tall four-legged stool and all the carriers would spend the last hour or two of each day sorting the next day's deliveries.

I would sit on my Dad's stool, my feet not reaching the ground, and talk to him or to his (and my) friends. Next to him on one side was Mr. Thornton, a short heavy set black man with the kindest smile, who was one of my Dad's best friends. Sometimes Mr. Thornton would buy me a soda and he would always kid around with me. On the other side of my Dad was Tony Calega, an Italian guy my father did odd jobs with on the side after work. Jobs like cutting lawns in the summer and in the winter they did interior painting at a Jewish temple that I think was in Pittsburgh's Squirrel Hill District. I'd go on these jobs most days too. I was the only kid I ever saw in the back of the post office and hanging out with the hundreds of working men always made me feel privileged to be there.

I was always close to my father as a boy and as a young man I still felt close to him but my 20s were spent far away. We visited but did not live close to one another. We narrowed it down to a few visits a year and phone calls every month or so. After my mother's death he remarried and I was never close to his 2nd wife. In my 20s I grew my own family. He died when I was 31, but I still see him occasionally in the faces of my brother and sons, and I hear him in our voices. I carry on his lifelong love of gardening and his easy way with people in how I live my life. I have a hundred more stories I could tell about him but they would all reflect the same ideas. I cannot call to mind more than a couple gifts my father bought for me, but what I can recall is how he integrated me in his daily life. I was never a chore for him. I was someone he loved and who loved him back. He was proud of me when I did good and patient with me when I did bad. He taught me the difference between the two. He taught me to be my own dog. He taught me to respect myself and to care for others. Though I faltered regularly (and still do) he taught me to get up again.

It's like I said before. My Father was a good man. He was no saint, but then no one is. Big love to you Dad wherever you are.

PART 2. GEORGIE

This story begins back in 1968. John Kennedy was dead almost 5 years and Robert Kennedy and Martin Luther King were both killed early that spring. The year before my mother, who I barely knew, had given up the ghost. My father's parents, who I had been very close to were both dead. Except for my Father most of my caregivers were gone. Daily we were all steeped in the tragedy of the Vietnam war and too young I felt that I had become inured to suffering, death, and dying. The Civil Rights Movement brought compulsory integration to our schools, and our communities into unwilling social revision. In seventh grade I was bussed to a new school in Pittsburgh's inner city, while blacks and whites clashed like cats and dogs in the streets and in the school hallways. I made a new friend that year, Georgie B. We were both twelve years old.

Georgie was smaller than me with flame red hair and more freckles than space between them. In retrospect I guess that he was of Irish or English extraction. Suffice it to say he was as white as a kid could be. He was small, but wiry and tough. His mother was a drunken whore (his words, not mine, I never met her) and there was no father figure in his concept of a family.

Maybe this is where things started going wrong for Georgie. His toughness came from a cross between premature self reliance and the hardened shell heart broken children learn to construct or crumble without. I think we had that in common, and so we became friends. This was the era of the Sharks and the Jets on the big screen, duking it out in West Side Story, our precursor to gangster rap. Even as kids we understood and embraced concepts like racism and sectarian violence, ideas like us and them, and keeping people who were different than us out of our neighborhood. It was a matter of identity and pride and face, or at least facade, in a world defined by 12 year olds.

The middle school I was bussed to was a brand new building five stories tall and built into a notch cut into one of Pittsburgh's steep hillsides. The front of the building faced Brighton Road, a wide four lane street with lots of traffic and city bus service that ran right past the school to downtown. The front of the first floor was at street level while the rear of the building was recessed into the hill and had another street level entry on the third floor facing Chateau Street. Chateau Street was a sharply inclined, cobblestone, two lane street barely bigger than an alley.

Outside of the school a steep concrete staircase connected both streets via half a dozen long flights of stairs. Offset by a dozen yards the staircase began again behind the school and climbed hundreds of steps from Chateau Street, through a precipitous wooded hillside, to Perry Avenue.

Those city steps were long and arduous and rose more than a dozen flights. At several intervals there were large landings with benches for resting. All of this was only accessible to pedestrian traffic . The landings were a favorite haunt of kids from the area. They could see the cops coming from quite a ways off. If trouble came they could escape by running up or down the stairs or by vaulting the railing and running off through the woods. This was a mostly black neighborhood and everyday after school Georgie had to climb these stairs, negotiating through the crowds of black boys that hung out there.

Georgie and I loved to play hooky from school and together we would usually skip a day or two each week. We'd go downtown where we'd spend our days walking the busy streets or hanging out around the river fronts, especially Point Park where the Monongahela and the Allegheny Rivers converged to form the Ohio. Another one of our most frequently visited places downtown were the Army Surplus stores on Liberty Avenue. Filled with knives, and canteens, and camouflage they were one of our favorite places to go. In the winter we'd spend time walking through the three big Department Stores: Horne's, Gimble's, and Kaufmann's, where we'd ride the escalators to the top floor and back down again, taking time to warm up thoroughly. Department stores at that time were highly entertaining for twelve year olds with holiday displays and high end consumer goods we could never imagine owning.

One time we were cruising Horne's Department Store and we'd stopped on the mezzanine level to look at record albums. Nearby were a bank of elevators and an exit leading to an elevated walkway that extended to a multistory parking garage. We picked out 10 or so albums by our favorite musicians in spite of not having more than bus fare in our pockets. We must have been obvious in our poverty and a store detective approached and laid hands on Georgie, intent on evicting us. Unplanned, but in perfect synchronicity, I snatched the albums and we both bolted out of the exit into the second floor of the parking garage. We ducked and dodged through the maze of cars, ran down the ramps and out onto the sidewalks lining Sixth Street. The crowds were thick and we ran through them until we were confident of our escape. We felt glorious and exhilarated. We laughed hysterically as we crossed the Sixth Street Bridge over the Allegheny River toward our neighborhood on Pittsburgh's North Shore.

We had no use at all for the albums and no where to play them. Neither of us could take them home. We stopped in the middle of the bridge at the apogee of the bridge's arc above the water and one at a time we sailed the albums like Frisbees, still unopened in their covers, out over the river to watch them land and float and slowly drift downstream. There was no sense of remorse from stealing, only a tremendous sense of relief and victorious triumph at our narrow escape. Afterwards we walked back toward school, me to catch a city bus and Georgie to walk the stairs to where ever he spent his nights.

Another day, and this part is one of the stories I usually don't like to tell, Georgie and I were cruising downtown . It must have been right before Easter. We went into the McCrory's Five and Dime, a big store off of Pittsburgh's Market Square. Outside there was a news stand and the guy who sold newspapers and periodicals always kept a wooden bushel basket full of soft pretzels and covered with newspaper. One of our favorite lunches was to share three pretzels, 25 cents each or three for 50 cents. We'd eat them on the benches of Market Square where the bag ladies would feed pigeons who flocked there by the hundreds.

At the time Five and Dime stores often sold baby chicks dyed gaudy colors for the Easter season. Like goldfish and baby turtles they were sold as disposable pets, holiday decorations, by the thousands, maybe by the millions. The vast majority were condemned before birth to backyard graves, being eaten by dogs and cats, or to a watery grave being flushed down the city's toilets.

We had so little money I can't imagine what possessed us to buy one, but we did. It came in a paper carton that folded closed, like the kind that Chinese take out food comes in. We carried it outside, down Fifth Avenue to Liberty, and from Liberty Avenue we made our way to Point Park. At the Park we let the chick run in the grass a bit. The weather was cold. The chick was despondent and not very active. We knew nothing of chickens. We put it back in the box and took it down to the river. At the rivers edge we opened the box and put the whole thing , like an open top life raft, into the Allegheny, where the current took it. We ran parallel to it along the side of the river as far as we could to the Point where the Monongahela merges to form the Ohio. The tiny box with the tiny chick in it was slowly swept away from us.

We were caught up in impulse and began to throw rocks at it. Eventually one stone found it's mark and sunk the box and the baby chick. Later we made our way home, me on the city bus, Georgie up the city stairs. I've always been haunted by that day. As an adult I've killed hogs and cows and sheep and deer and hundreds of chickens all without remorse, but that one baby chick has haunted me for 50 years. What has haunted me most about it is when I recall that story and ask "who am I?" I am unhappy with the answer.

I didn't see Georgie all that next summer but when the new school year started in the fall we were reunited. We hung out together for a month or two, then he disappeared. There was a rumor that he had been shot. No one knew what really happened until several months later when Georgie showed up back at school. His head was covered in peach fuzz except for a bald spot on one side where powder burns from a point blank gun shot left a couple of inches of scar tissue no longer capable of growing hair. It turned out that one day Georgie was climbing the city stairs and as he passed through a group of boys one of them put a small caliber gun to his head and pulled the trigger. This was in an era unlike today and a teenager with a gun was uncommon. No witnesses came forward and no one was held accountable. Every day Georgie still had to walk home up the same city stairs to whatever sort of place he spent his nights. Certainly by this point things were going very wrong for Georgie.

He changed deeply after the shooting and he and I didn't hang out together much. He came to school less frequently and eventually stopped coming at all. Over the next few years of high school I heard a few rumors about him but not much. The last time I heard about Georgie was probably when I was in tenth or eleventh grade. Someone said he had developed a scam hustling guys in porn stores along Liberty Avenue not far from the Army Surplus stores we used to frequent.

The way the story was told to me was Georgie would lure guys from inside the stores with promises of sex and together they'd go to the service alley behind the store. There he'd beat them and rob them. Like I said he was small but he was tough. I don't know where he lived by then or if he still had to climb those city stairs. That was the last I ever heard about Georgie.

I guess the story didn't surprise me as much as it should have. He never really stood much of a chance. Looking back it's easy to try to find a pivotal moment where things went wrong for Georgie, but I don't think there was one. I think there were a million times things went bad for him. We all love to think of the resiliency of the human spirit. We love to tell and hear stories where a hero proudly proclaims "I am".

But not every story goes that way. There are people in the world who don't stand much more of a chance than a fluorescent yellow Dime

Store peep. Maybe when we hear their stories we should ask ourselves "Who am I?".

I'm reminded of the meditation "Wu Wei." There are several translations from Chinese, my favorite among them is "without effort or will." It is exemplified by the inexorable path each raindrop follows to make its way to the ocean. Without effort, or intent, or will power every raindrop finds its way home, washing away mountains, cutting canyons, dissolving continents. It can be held in suspended animation as ice or surge as a driving flood, but it cannot be stopped. It possesses no desire, or will, no animosity toward the land, and wages no war. Without organization every raindrop works in concert and harmony seeking the ocean, following the raindrops that have gone before, and easing the path for raindrops that will follow.

I have studied on Wu Wei for many years. I have talked about it with friends and planted it as a seed, but it is only half the story. By the time a raindrop finds the ocean, the identity of the drop is lost but the full measure of water is retained. Much as a raindrop is drawn to the ocean it is also at home in the sky as a cloud. it is at home at rest and in motion, as vapor and as liquid, in a wave, a fogbank, a redwood tree, and in you and me. It is at home in the surge of a tsunami and in the flow of mother's milk. All without effort or will or desire.

While there is nothing a raindrop can teach us, we can learn from it the way of the world, and our path in it.

When I lived in the redwood forest I loved the fog. It would saturate the world. It was cool, often chilly, sometimes cold. It reduced my field of vision but it also hid me from the world. Living in the Lilliputian world of the redwoods I could achieve that most precious of states, I became anonymous. I could achieve a loss of identity while at the same time find myself complete in harmony with my environment.

I belonged in the forest as much as the deer and the ferns. I was wetted by the dew and dried by the sun. I was as much at home sleeping in the duff in the heart of an ancient tree as were the scorpions and centipedes that lived there with me. I became comfortable in the deep woods and in my own skin at the same time.

In the forest, in the meadows, at the shore, I was home everywhere, probably for the first time in my life. What a great discovery it was at 20, to lose myself, and find myself simultaneously.

The illusion of my separateness fell away without trying. Without effort. Without desire. Wu Wei.

JANUARY, 2015
MOONBEAMS

I don't know if you saw the moon this morning. It was full and brilliant and silver white. When I started walking in the early dark, it was still a hand's breadth above the western horizon, dodging in and out of a sky of broken clouds. I thought of the pact we made when I last saw you, that every time we saw the moon we would be together in our hearts. In our heart.

I would have slept til five this morning but someone in a nearby bunk had their alarm set for 4 AM. Poor Frank has a hard time sleeping and wears a mask at night to feed him air and moisture so that his apnea doesn't choke him in his sleep. His machine is so loud that he cannot discern his alarm and he sleeps right through it. Not so for a dozen other guys who get up to shuffle to the toilets to pee, and to curse Frank, and then shuffle back to their bunk.

I got up and tapped Frank's foot to wake him up. He shut off the alarm and went back to sleep. I wondered if it hurt his scalp to sleep on such tightly plaited, rubber banded, nappy hair. His head looks like it's covered in fuses. It might hurt, but it doesn't keep him awake.

So I was already up and unlike Frank and so many other inmates here who have learned to sleep away as many years as they can, I could not go back to bed. I dressed and headed outside into the frosted yard. I pulled my knitted cap low in the back, to keep my neck warm.

While making my way to the walking track, bright beneath the sodium lights, I could see the moon. With still a few hours before it set, it came and went behind a broken cloud cover. I could see my breath. I thought of you. I thought right now you might be laying in bed. You may have woken up in the early morning dark to worry about what is to come and wondering what to do, who to be. The brightness of the moon shining in the window next to your bed may have woken you up.

You might be thinking of me. You might be missing me. I hope instead you are sleeping peacefully. I hope the down comforter is pulled up around your neck and you are cozy and warm. I hope your breathing is calm and soft and relaxed. I hope you are at peace in your dreams. I think of the thousands of early mornings I have woken up next to you in the dark.

While I walked the moon broke through the canopy of clouds, stabbing the dark sky, before being swallowed up again.

I plod along the walking track, lapping the yard. The moon reminds me of how it was when I lay with you, your back to me and my arm across you. Breathing in your molecules. I am forever infused with your scent. It is buried in my blood and bonded into my brain.

I flux.

At times I miss you so much my heart breaks and the tears flow.

I flux.

I know we cannot be separated. We can never be apart. Time and distance will never separate us.

I flux.

Like the moon that comes and goes behind the sky of broken clouds.

I flux.

APRIL, 2015
BLACK KITCHEN FRANK

Black Kitchen Frank's bunk was/is across the aisle from mine. He slept each night of the past seven months five feet away from me. Every day he would stand an arm's length away from me for the head counts the guards perform periodically throughout the day. Just a month or so ago he became a regular 4th in our evening card games. He died last night while refereeing a basketball game. He simply stopped in his jog up and down the court long enough to say "Oh no" then dropped to the tarmac like a ton of bricks. His black and white striped referee shirt stood out like a caution sign among the gray and green prison clothes of the inmates who rushed to help him when he fell. CPR and mouth to mouth failed to resuscitate him. He went down hard and stayed there.

Frank was a sweet man. Kind. Gentle. Quick to smile. He spent hundreds of hours cutting potato chip bags into tiny strips of silver, blue, and red foil. He folded these into long zig-zag chains then sewed them together to fashion purses, belts, and wristbands for friends and family. Last Christmas he asked me what my wife's name and favorite colors were.

"Diane" I told him "purple and pink". He got enough purple from a discarded Cheese Puffs bag to cut out her name and worked it into a bracelet braided from an unraveled blanket. He gave it to me to give to her, symptomatic of his generous nature .

I made him soup several times, my specialty soup of Chicken Ramen and garlic sliced paper thin, with a tiny splash of olive oil. A culinary delight in this shithole.

When Frank was lying on the ground the guards came out and sent us all back to the housing unit. We watched through plate glass windows as the CPR continued. It took almost an hour for the ambulance to arrive. The general consensus was that if a guard had been attacked there would of been a SWAT team deployed within five minutes. Who can tell? This prison is a giant clusterfuck, a discombobulation, a cursed plan on cursed ground.

Sometimes Frank and I would drink hot tea together. When I asked , he told me he was down more than ten years with still several more to go. On the outside he had worked as a bouncer at a nightclub in Indiana. The owners were accused of dealing cocaine. The Feds organized and threatened enough snitches to indict 50 people. The way it works is they put the squeeze on a couple of people who are given the option of providing information "leading to the arrest and conviction" of a number of others. If they comply their own sentences are reduced, if they don't, then their lives are destroyed.

The people they testify against are presumed guilty and given the same choices. There is absolutely no incentive for the police to establish the truth, if a person is innocent. In fact the opposite is true. Police and prosecutors at every level are judged by the number of convictions and years of sentences handed out on their arrests and prosecutions. To prove someone innocent is counter intuitive and self defeating. It would be impossible to contrive a more inaccurate or destructive system.

Police investigations are reduced to a series of intimidations and pitting people against each other. Real guilt or innocence is irrelevant. Only arrests and convictions, and long sentences matter, and many, many convictions are based on no evidence at all, except the testimony of coerced witnesses struggling to save their own lives. Sadly, this is standard operating procedure and it fills the prisons with people who won't sacrifice others to save themselves. It does nothing to improve society, further public safety, or accomplish the original objectives of the law.

We incentivize the police and prosecutors and judges and legislators to build careers on the number of years of incarceration they can dole out. We equate incarceration with justice, deify overt police militarization and violence against the general populace, and reorient the military industrial complex to train its sights on our own citizenry. We live in a country with 5% of the world's population and 25% of the world's prisoners. One in every three adult black men will serve time in jail/prison in their lifetime. In the the last 4 years Americans have served 10 million years of prison time. Frank was one man in this miasma of statistics.

About an hour after they took Franks body away, they showed up to pack out his stuff. One guard and 2 or 3 inmates showed up. They had a laundry cart for his clothes which are government property, a plastic box for his personal effects, which amounted to a few books, a small sheaf of papers, a plastic cup and bowl, a small radio, a couple lanyards with crosses on them, some half finished craft projects, and some family photos. He had a wife and two daughters that I know of.

One daughter had recently received a masters degree and the other a CDL license for long haul trucking. He showed me pictures of his mom once. I wonder if she is still alive. All his possessions fit in the the plastic tub with room to spare. About the size of a bushel basket, it represented the sum total of ten years of his life. everything else was thrown away except for for a few packs of sardines and a couple of instant soups that were given to a new guy that arrived yesterday. Welcome home.

I wrote more than I thought I would. It dawned on me I wrote this for two reasons. First not a handful of people who read this will understand what it means that Frank spent the last ten years of his life in prison. It can't be imagined, or visualized, or written about accurately. Frank's incarceration and length of sentence, the hardship and pain to him and his family, was disproportionate to the crime he was accused of. I want to blame people. Legislators who build careers being "tough on crime". The courts and police who are the dogs to these masters.. Especially I want to blame the complacent public who would rather not see the truth and do something to change it. The public who are willing to let an oppressive police state and the profiteers who rule it run roughshod over millions of lives, until it catches them and they find they are too powerless to resist.

The second reason I wrote this is to pay homage to Frank. How his heart lasted as long as it did is a testimony to his strength. He was kind. He was generous. He lived by the faith he professed. He was moral. He was gracious. He smiled easily. He was a good person.

He was my friend.

PART 3. SONOMA

When I first arrived in the Coastal Range of Sonoma County, California it was in the spring of 1975, during the Lenten season, auspicious timing for my personal resurrection.

I was raised in an inner city environment. A neighborhood of perhaps 40,000 Italian and Polish immigrants, bordered on one side by the white suburb called Bellevue, and on three sides by a black urban neighborhood of several hundreds of thousands known as the Lower Northside. I was a city kid. During my childhood "the Woods" consisted of some trees and weeds and poison ivy mixed with discarded appliances, vehicle parts, and construction debris. It was a city block long and wide.

We called it "The Backies". It separated the cobblestone alley behind my house from Rt. 65, the Ohio River Boulevard, a major traffic artery linking downtown Pittsburgh with the communities and industry that lined the north shore of the Ohio River.

I remember once as a kid our family, along with many others, walked to a pedestrian foot bridge over the boulevard to watch and wave to JFK who passed below us in an open topped convertible and who according to a family legend born that day, waved back to my teenage sister. I was only eight, but it dawned on me at the time that I could have hit him with a brick. On the other side of the highway a steep shale cliff fell a hundred feet to the flat floodplain of the Ohio River. At the foot of the cliff were a dozen sets of railroad track, then a broad expanse of heavy industry lining the river's edge.

As kids we were expressly forbidden to go to the river, especially to swim, so naturally we gravitated towards there. We had paths through the "backies" behind our house, a favorite place to dodge through the highway traffic on Route 65, and on the far side a wide enough shoulder to walk on, all the way to the McKee's Rocks Bridge, a major steel arch bridge spanning the river. The shale cliffs were too steep to negotiate but under the bridge there was a large storm sewer drainage pipe built to carry runoff from the highway during periods of heavy rain. It fell for about 50 yards at a 45 degree angle and was constructed of four foot sections of about three feet in diameter.

Each piece interlocked with the next, the bottom of one fitting into the expanded lip of the piece below it. Usually we'd climb up and down the outside of the pipe, though it was a rite of passage for all boys was to make the descent on the inside. This entailed pressing one's hands and feet against the pipes sides and holding yourself above the grease slick algae that lined the pipe's bottom.

One slip could mean a meteoric plummet, losing acres of skin, and being ejected into an open air settling tank at the the pipe's discharge end. It was like a rock tumbler for children but with the added elements of infectious disease and humiliation.

Acquiring a safe descent, we'd play on the trains loaded with industrial freight of coal and coke and pelleted pig iron bound for the mills, or consumer goods such as rail carriers of new automobiles. Immediately beyond the tracks was the industrial zone, the final frontier that separated us from the river.

To the left (upstream) was an abandoned manufacturing facility with peeling yellow letters painted on the side spelling out "Screw and Bolt Co." Beyond that were the massive, blackened, sandstone block walls of Western Penitentiary, the stone peeling like the bark of a sycamore tree from the corrosive air and rain.

To the right (downstream) were large brown fields and railroad track sidings with tipples for loading and off loading barges and train cars into each other. Directly in front of us was the Sanitation Plant, processor of Pittsburgh's household waste, effluence, and industrial runoff.

Just downstream were large concrete escarpments stabilizing the banks and holding in place large diameter storm sewer pipes for jettisoning raw sewage overloads in periods of heavy rain.

This concrete beach was our favorite place to swim. The concrete apron extended well below the waterline and though coated with a combination of industrial and fecal goop, at least there were no pieces of sharp metal or rubble to snag on.

Swimming there always resulted in a head to toe rash, akin to full body hives. We had to leave at least an hour to get home to give the reaction time to subside.

One of the most durable elements to pass through the sewers were the heavy latex condoms so common to the era. They lined the river bank for miles below the sewage plant, distorted by their short but vigorous use and the long tumble through the sewer system, before their ignominious deposition on the shore. We called them "Allegheny Whitefish," though I have no idea why.

One of our favorite games was to pick them up with sticks and chase each other with them. Few sounds were as satisfying as the resounding thwack of sodden latex on bare skin, as those deflated party balloons found their marks. Sweet memories of childhood and summer. We were like post-apocalyptic Tom Sawyers.

Growing up in such an industrial setting had its positives and negatives. As the Vietnam war wound down so did the market for Pittsburgh's steel. At the same time mills in other countries increased their output and undercut our prices. The steel city was fast becoming the poster child for the rust belt, just as I was coming of age and leaving. It was like climbing out of a burning car.

A couple of years of living on the road and the sea expanded my horizons and increased my sense of worldliness. I gained a broader concept of humanity and of America, of the people and the place. It seemed to me that the world was expressed as a great dichotomy, good and bad, beautiful and ugly, life and death.

On the road I met the best and the worst in people. On the water I was introduced to the duality of the infinite beauty of the ocean and at the same time the destruction of that beauty. There were incomparable sunrises and sunsets on the water. There were millions of iridescent, fully inflated, purple Portuguese men of war floating in lines three feet wide and stretching to the horizon. There were giant ocean sunfish skimming algae from sea's surface. In juxtaposition there were the offshore oil fields off the coast of Louisiana and Texas. There was the dead zone caused by the pollution from the Houston River viewed from the water looking inland. There was the wanton and cavalier slaughter *en masse* of sea life by the trawlers I worked on.

An average day's catch might range from 200-500 pounds of shrimp. Sometimes more, often less. To affect that catch we'd trawl 24 hours a day, dragging two nets, each 150 feet wide with a heavy tickler chain stretched across the mouth of each, bouncing across the sea floor, leveling and killing everything in its path. A path 300 feet wide and 50 to 100 miles long each day.

I was introduced to hundreds of species of aquatic life I'd never seen before, all of it as it lay dying on the after deck. To engage in this sort of work one must harden the senses, deny the reality, then desensitize our relationship with nature and with life.

We would regularly kill 400 to 500 pounds of of sea life to catch 200 pounds of shrimp, all of it dumped on deck and allowed to die, sorted through, then scuttled overboard. Only on the last two or three days of each trip were we allowed to keep the most valuable food fishes; pompano, flounder, and red snapper, and only then if we had ice to waste.

The novelty of the life and work wore off after a while, the sense of adventure diluted with experience, and the weight of the truth lay heavy on me. By the end of my second stint on the water I was in need of joy. To that end I headed to New Orleans.

One cannot live in the streets of the French Quarter during Mardi Gras, sleep on the levies and in the cemeteries, and pass ten days at the biggest party in America without having stories to tell. Suffice it to say that for me it wasn't joy I found there.

It was more a celebration of inebriation, an exercise in excess, and an expression of debauchery that added to the bad taste in my mouth.

I was done with it by Fat Tuesday and on Ash Wednesday I was headed west, as so many before me have, called by the Siren of California.

The great promise, the sense of new beginnings, the titillation of the unknown, all calling me to the home I did not yet know.

I headed north through the bayous, then west on interstate 10 across the great expanse of northern Texas and the deserts of the southwest, rolling into Los Angeles. From there north on highways 1 and 101, falling in love with our left coast. The farms, the shore, the mountains, the wildlife, the big trees, and the people. Landing in Berkeley was like landing on a hot plate.

I've spent a lot of time in Berkeley on subsequent visits and learned to love it, but late in my 19th year the congestion of people, the in-my-face effrontery of the politics, and the compression of humanity were all salt in the wounds I'd been protecting. I no longer needed triage care, I was primed for the cure. It would take place in an ancient forest 100 miles to the north. In a wilderness of trees, meadows, and rocky shore I would walk off my burdens losing my luggage along the way. In the mountain streams and the cold Pacific surf I would wash away the grime. The California sun and star lit nights would illuminate my shadowy places.

I didn't know any of this at the time. My arrival in the redwoods would mark a pivotal change in my life. Knowing only that I was tired of everything human, I sought solace in the wilderness. As it always does the wilderness lay waiting for my return to a place I had never been before.

JANUARY, 2015
BUTTERFLY KISSES

Out walking the track tonight beneath the glare of the sodium lights, I see the moon a hand's width above the eastern horizon. It's still just a little flat down low on the left and looks to be 4-5 days shy of full. Every moon reminds me of you and this one is no exception. I think of this same midwinter moon 36 years ago when you and I were hitch hiking and we slept beneath it in the towering redwoods just north of where the Russian

River spills into the Pacific. We were young then and we would sleep so tight together, face to face. We would share each other's breath. Our faces were so close that our eyelashes would brush each others cheeks and we called it butterfly kisses.

That was 36 midwinter moons ago. Two kids ago. Ten houses ago. That was being broke a hundred times ago and being flush a hundred times ago. Being happy and sad a million times ago. That was 50 vacations ago, a dozen cars ago, careers ago. That time beneath big trees cultivating big love was 100 arguments ago, 101 make ups ago, 10,000 miles walked ago, a million miles by thumb and car and plane and boat ago. That was 15 countries ago and 40 states ago. That was illnesses ago and injuries ago and recoveries ago. That was a 1,000 books ago and 10,000 poems ago. That was colleges and trade schools ago. That was fruit trees and gardens ago. That was iris' and daylilies ago. That was old generations dying ago and new generations being born ago.

That time was police raids ago and jail times ago. That time was Christmas' and Thanksgivings and birthdays ago. That time was a bucket of tears and decades of laughter ago. That time was more than 10,000 nights together ago. Still it is not enough of you for me. There will be many more moons to come and each one will call you to mind again.

I dream of a time when we lie so close that we share each other's breath again. I dream of your eyelashes brushing my cheeks again and of my eyelashes brushing your cheeks again. I dream of whispering to you again "butterfly kisses."

OCTOBER, 2015

ANGRY MR. M

I've been down more than a year now. Two weeks ago was our wedding anniversary and the beginning of my second year of incarceration. Diane visited me two weekends ago on Saturday and Monday. It is the highlight of my day/month/life to be with her. Since her last visit she has really been on my mind. I escape by thinking of her. I touch base with reality by conjuring her up in my head. It's much different from the consumptive thoughts of new love. It is even more persistent. Less mysterious. More consistent. Deeper knowledge. I know clearly what I'm missing.

This past Saturday morning was much warmer than it has been lately. I walked to the chow hall for breakfast while it was still dark. The sky to the west was a low, heavy bank of clouds stretching from north to south, sharply defining an incoming weather front. To the east it was still clear and I could see Venus bright in the dark blue sky with Mars down to the left and faintly, Saturn right above it. They look to almost be touching. They are 350 million miles apart. So much is perspective.

After breakfast I met up with a friend, Mr. M. We usually walk together but for the last week or so I've been walking with other inmates or by myself. Mr. M. cast disparaging remarks about this absence. Mr. M. has anger issues. He is constantly doing "Coping with Anger" workbooks or "Anger Management" classes or writing reports on books like "Dealing with Anger".

They all affect him profoundly. He is profoundly pissed off for having to work on his anger. That is about par for the course living in a therapeutic community. Out of 100 alcoholics, junkies and addicts I live with he is the angriest. He continues to rant on a variety of subjects and people while we walk. I tune him out and instead listen to the grey limestone gravel crunch beneath our feet.

As we round the track and face the east I see the first light glowing from beneath the horizon. In spite of Mr. M.'s diatribe against the world my mind wanders. I'm thinking of Diane again. In the visitor's room we are allowed one kiss and hug when she arrives and one kiss and hug when she leaves. The rest of the time we sit in chairs on opposite sides of a low table. I love to bury my nose in the nape of her neck and inhale her molecules during our hug. It has to be quick. The guards will come down hard on you if they define your behavior as inappropriate.

So I inhale deeply, infusing myself with as many of her molecules as possible. Maybe that's why she's been on my mind so much lately. Maybe her molecules are churning around in my brain.

Mr. M. keeps on bitching with the regularity of clockwork. Now he's complaining about not having any friends. I suggest it's because he's a pain in the ass. He agrees without hesitation and laughs about it. That's a good sign. The walking and talking are getting him to laugh. Second lap and we are headed west again. The sky is dark and solid and low. It is thick and heavy like snow clouds, though the air is too warm for that. Now Mr. M. is pissed off about something else (he never really quit).

I shut out his noise. I think of Diane again. We've been together since 1978. That's a long time to sleep together. Even if you subtract a couple years for business trips, separate travel, nights we've fought and slept in the guest bed, prison , and other places, that still is more than 12,500 night together. I must have inhaled pounds of her molecules in that time.

Mr. M. and I round the far end of the track and turn east again. as we do the first beams of light begin to illuminate the belly of the cloud cover. First it tinges the edges a sort of pink. Then within moments the light progresses across the entire underside of the sky turning it orange and coral and peach. I stop and tell Mr. M. to shut up for a minute. He stares at the ground when he walks and recites his caustic liturgy, but now he stops and looks up.

The colors of the sky compliment the autumnal shades of the maples and oaks that surround the track. Every shade of red and yellow and orange infuse the sky and the trees and the air in between. The saturation of color is perfect and brilliant and fleeting. Even Mr. M. is speechless. In silence we begin walking again. The only sound is the crunching of the gravel beneath our shoes. I'm thinking.

I can't find the words to say exactly how it is, but the same way the dawn has lit up the gray overcast sky above this prison, thinking of Diane lights me up. When I am gray she colors my world.

LIFE AMONG THE REDWOODS

In 1975 I arrived in Sonoma County, California, about five miles north of Jenner-by-the-Sea, where the Russian River pours into the Pacific Ocean.

In Berkeley I'd met Ed, who owned an interest in a large, steep tract of redwood forest and grassy meadows in the Coastal Range. It was a series of thousand foot hills and deep canyons running out to the Pacific Coastal Highway and just beyond to the ocean.

I struck a loose deal with Ed in which I would stay on his place and help with some chores and in exchange he'd bring me a box of groceries every other week or so. There were no buildings or electric services, no developed water system save for a convenient year-round spring that crossed the access road. For a toilet, there was an outhouse.

At the head of the biggest canyon, opening to the west, in a three acre level clearing where he would one day build a house, Ed parked a small, silver, tow-behind Airstream camper trailer. He and his wife used it on the rare occasions that they stayed overnight. It was the rainy season when I first arrived and they said I could use it anytime I liked as long as it was clean and tidy when they arrived.

I spent a few nights in it early on, but I was too stifled by it's confinement. While living on the road, in the preceding few years, I had slept outside hundreds of nights, and long ago I had abandoned my pup tent.

My preference for sleeping on the ground and in the open gave me an intimate relationship with the night and an awareness of place, even while asleep, that is crucial to survival and safety for a transient person. I carried a small tarp and a lightweight cotton bag. I could fall asleep on top of or inside the sleeping bag. When I anticipated a heavy dew or fog I could spread the tarp for a ground cloth and fold it over me. When it rained I could roll myself up in it. In severe weather I could huddle, seated on my sleeping roll and cocoon myself in the tarp to wait it out.

I usually slept light and woke often throughout the night learning to love the sleepy glimpses of the stars. I also learned a deep appreciation of my immersion in the weather. Living in the redwood forest where the weather is usually mild, this trait became a wonderful privilege, a sense of the here and now throughout every night. To this day I measure the quality of my life in direct correlation to the number of nights I get to sleep outside.

The chores I did for the owners only took a few hours a week. Things like keeping the driveway clear of fallen sticks and making sure the culverts stayed unobstructed and drained well. Sometimes I did a little mowing and once I built a 16-foot gate from redwood lumber scraps, in the shape of a rectangle with a rising sun in the lower left and sunbeams radiating outward. It wasn't a gate to stop animals or people who could simply walk around it. It wouldn't stop anyone who was determined to come in. It was the kind of gate that implied a desire for privacy. Less of a "KEEP OUT" gate and more of a "Please don't intrude" gate.

On the weekends when Ed would show up I'd help with whatever projects he had going on. Ed wasn't much of a laborer, he was an intellectual who enjoyed tinkering and he didn't demand much of me. The biggest purpose I served for him was to be a presence on his property and this suited me fine. I could spend almost all my time as I pleased. Ed enjoyed the natural beauty of the environment as did I, so he too appreciated a light touch on the landscape.

I developed methods to live in the forest that precluded intrusive developments. I was content to catch spring water in a plastic bucket for washing and drinking near my camp. Over the course of the next nine months I learned where the drinking springs were in the areas I ranged. The meadows and forest edges were populated with sheep, wild pigs, and deer so I chose springs deep in the forest where they did not frequent or contaminate. Most larger animals shun the thick canopy of the redwoods, which are generally devoid of foodstuffs for them. They preferred the edge environs and transitional areas where the forest was sparse and sunlight hit the ground.

By following the streams and moving up the canyons I became adept at looking for the tiny tributaries trickling out of the forest and following them to their source. I'd scoop out a hollow space with my hands a foot or two from where it emerged from the ground and I could be assured of clean water to drink wherever I walked. Sometimes I would hide a cleaned out can from my store-bought groceries nearby to have a cup handy on demand.

How fine it was on a hot summer's day to slip into a darkened glade, the shade heavy and cool, and to sit on the forest floor beneath the giant trees, sipping water purified and sanctified by the ground it percolated from.

I had three methods for my ablutions. First was the bucket at the spring. The driveway was more than half a mile long and notched into a steep, heavily wooded hillside. Leaving my camp the gravel driveway rose to meet the main ranch road climbing perhaps 200 feet in elevation. On the way up, the hillside fell precipitously to the right and rose steeply on the left. Halfway up there was a small but constant spring on the high side of the road. With a shovel I cut a depression into the bank big enough to accommodate a plastic five-gallon bucket and a wide flat paver stone for it to stand on. The bucket caught and collected the trickle and stayed over flowing except when I would lift it down. I usually washed in cold water, standing in the road. It was a big woods and there was no one to see me.

Yesterday I was talking to Diane and she reminded me of the nonlinear nature of time. Writing about this now I am seated facing the grey steel lockers in my prison cell but I am smelling the wet clay of Sonoma County where the water collected in the white plastic bucket. I smell the cool damp air of the redwood forest understory. In this moment I am free.

The second method I would use to wash was to walk downhill instead of up. Downhill in any direction led to water. Behind my camp, headed inland, I could follow old remnants of logging roads down to the creek. Still fairly high in elevation, the creek was small enough to jump across and fell quickly in a series of small pools and waterfalls. The water was cold and fast-moving, still covered in many places by the canopy of trees. I would often see the tiny coastal range deer here and the tracks of the wild pigs in this area. There was enough water to bathe in and to wash my clothes in the pools, enough wilderness to nap in the sun while my clothes dried, hung on the bushes.

This area was still close to my camp, no more than half a mile laterally and a couple hundred feet lower. Access was easy. On hot days it was exhilarating to stick my sweaty head under an icy cascade and revel in the pummeling after a long walk afield.

The greatest luxury in bathing available to me was to leave camp, drop down the western flank of the canyon, very steep but negotiable on foot, then follow the creek to the ocean. The canyon floor fell quickly and the walls were steep, so that landslides and fallen timber created a plethora of log jams and rock piles to work around and through.

At close to sea level the creek was traversed by a one lane bridge, part of the ranch's access road, then a little farther on it passed under a two lane bridge beneath Highway 101, the PCH. Beyond that it entered a thicket of brush 10-15 feet tall for perhaps 100 yards. On the far side of the thicket it exited onto the stony beach and dissipated, coming to an ambiguous ending, percolating through the rocks into the sea. The brush thicket was dense, so tight it could only be entered by ducking low and walking in the stream bed.

Wading in it, I would immediately disappear from view from the highway, from the beach, from everywhere and everyone. Deep in the bushes, slowed in its path to the sea, the stream spread wide, from 10 feet it broadened to 50 feet across. As the water slowed the clay held in suspension precipitated and the wide shallow pond had a silky grained mud bottom. In the summer on the sunny days the water would heat to tepid. I loved to walk to the beach and soak for long periods, hidden in the brushy thicket. I could hear the highway, sometimes people on the beach, always the surf, yet I was totally hidden, the entire scene perfectly private.

When I arrived in March, it was the wet season. There were rain showers most days and most nights. Throughout the clearing where I camped were mixed hardwoods, mostly oaks and bay trees. Beyond them, in every direction, was redwood forest. About 150 yards from the camper, on the lip of the canyon, was a grove of redwoods. A dozen secondary growth trees grew in roughly a circle with their branches knitted together all the way to the ground.

They were big trees to a boy like me from the east, three feet in diameter and 80 feet tall.

Hidden in the center of the circle was an enormous stump, 15 feet high and more than 20 feet across at the cut, even wider at ground level. The base was hollow, as many of the big redwoods are, and it was probably why it was cut so high. From what I've read since, it was probably somewhere between 1500 and 2000 years old.

I explored the grove and stump thoroughly. Redwoods are so resistant to rot that it had changed little since being cut. It hadn't really died entirely. All the secondary growth trees were sprouted from its roots, It still remained integrated in a literal web of life. Tiny shoots sprouted from its bark well over a century since the main trunk had been cut.

On top of the stump the cut had two large flats. One at a lower level where the notch to direct the fall had been incised and a second slightly higher flat from the felling cut.

Between them, a band of shattered splinters protruded, marking the zone of wood still uncut when the preponderance of weight in the tree proved to be more than it could hold up and gave way, snapping and shattering as the behemoth keeled over.

I loved to climb the stump and sleep on the flats or sit there and look out over the canyon and sea below me. I would often lie in the deep shade and stare up into the trees around me and the sky beyond. I stowed my gear in the hollow below and when it rained I slept there too.

It was extremely dark inside, in the daytime and of course even more so at night. Many times I would wake in the night and have no idea of the time without stepping outside to see the sky. I never built fires inside or on top of the stump and so learned the special nature of spending the evening and night in the forest without a fire. If I wanted a campfire to watch or cook on I built one in the meadow by the camper. Anyone walking near the grove would have no clue to my presence there.

To this day, much as I love to sit by a fire I still carry the lessons learned there, to be in the forest as daylight transitions to night and to appreciate the light, the twilight and the dark equally, without a fire.

It is now Sunday Morning. I've been working on this part of the story off and on for several days. I'll write more in the coming weeks. I struggled quite a bit with writing about the stump. The privilege of living there and the relationship I developed with those trees and that place are difficult for me to express in words. At times the language seems so inadequate, so impotent in my desire to convey the experience and the impressions I gained there, but on a selfish level this writing serves me as a vehicle of transcendence. It's like Diane reminded me of the other day, the true nature of time is nonlinear.

MARCH, 2015

We've had several snow storms in the past month and some bitter cold. This kept everyone confined to our housing unit. 130 guys too close together, too much of the time. Too much talking, shouting, swearing, farting, and snoring. It fluxes between oppressive and comical. However the last three days have been fabulous, sunny, bright, warm, near 60 degrees, with a slight warm southern breeze. Everyone has flocked outside to walk, run, play basketball, and bask in the sun. It is the cure! Spirits are improved as has the smell of the housing unit. The foot deep snow of 4 days ago has melted except in the hidden nooks and crannies. No telling if we'll have more wintry weather, but for now life is better in the monkey cage!

A few anecdotal things about the people I live with. It's easy to think of them as "convicts" but like all prejudices, that term doesn't really describe the person. Each man is his own story. I've tried to tell some small bits about several guys in previous posts. There are some commonalities though. Many people in prison either adopt or are given pseudonyms or nicknames. I live with guys who go by Street, D Block, OT, T, G Money, Father Time, Crazy Ted, Brother Young, the Rev., Chicken F., Slim, Scrappy, Country, Levi aka Eli, Dexter, Speedy, Big J, Smiley, Bull City, Scooter, Easy E, Stunner, White Mike, Black Mike, White Kitchen Frank, Black Kitchen Frank, Mamout, Drew-El, Jimmy Vinny, Wrinkle Dick aka Harry Twatter, the Nerds, Vee, Tits, and Silent Killer (named after his card playing style).

Pseudonyms provide a degree of anonymity and also protection from snitches. You can imagine this testimony in court " Yes, Your honor I did see Wrinkle Dick break a law while in Gilmer Prison. His real name your Honor? I believe it's Harry Twatter."

So these are the guys I live with, eat with, sleep near, shit near. Shower next to, listen to snore and fart, hear argue and curse, and put a hand on the shoulder of when the loneliness breaks them for a moment. They are all just men, both good and bad in each one, multi faceted like men everywhere.

Lately I play chess two evenings a week with the "Chess Club" . Chicken is just learning, I've played off and on all my life. Some guys in the club have played many hundreds of hours a year for decades. Chess is a big deal in prison. Competition is stiff and I'm learning a lot. Lately I've been learning King and Queen Gambit openings.

Another couple evenings a week I play cards, usually with Chicken F, Silent Killer, and Harry Twatter. We play a game that's called "Suicide Rummy". It takes about an hour and a half a game and requires two decks of cards for four players. To make the game more interesting we enhance the deck with extra jokers and we cheat. I've not played cards as an adult before so it's been fun learning and I'm getting good enough to cheat really well. There's no gambling so the cheating is good-natured.

We talk and joke quite a bit while we play and we sing quite a bit too. Silent Killer rarely talks but he laughs often and is pleasant company. He's in his mid fifties and missing many of his teeth from years of methamphetamine use, but he's powerfully built, and a devout Christian. He's also madly in love with his wife and misses her enormously. We have this in common. Harry Twatter is 31, the age of my youngest son. He suffers from PTSD stemming from military service in equatorial Africa where he did things that are easiest to live with on heroin. He's a big reader, and sometimes I walk with him.

The prison system does nothing good for him or his root problems, but he seems to be lightening up as time passes. I cannot help but fear for him. I try to balance the fear by hoping for the best for him. Chicken

F is the age of my oldest son. He is hilariously funny, a bluegrass musician (guitar) and has a thick hillbilly accent. The F. is short for either Fighter, because he's in prison for cock fighting, or Fucker, because it's funny to call him chicken fucker, just depending on the speaker's mood. I've taught Chicken F. to play chess and he and I are the only white guys in the chess club.

Along those lines I'm also the only white guy invited into the pool room. There is a very small room with a very small beat-to-hell pool table. The felt on the table is as smooth as broken pavement and the rails are lifeless and sag like used condoms. Still, it has all its balls and four warped cues. There's also a television, and a broken treadmill in the room. The room is run by a black clique, but once the snow began to accumulate outside, I was invited to use the treadmill. I usually go once, sometimes twice a day and walk 15 minutes on the treadmill and sometimes I stay for another hour to talk and kid around with the crew. I particularly like to make fun of the TV shows they watch, primarily soap operas and black reality shows.

I had no idea there were so many black reality shows on TV. I've also come to see the broken treadmill as a perfect analogy for Prison life. It is an endlessly repetitive exercise that goes nowhere, is broken and no one is interested in fixing it. Once you're on it you have to get what you can out of it and try not to watch too much bad TV while you're at it.

MAY, 2015
A TRIP TO THE HOSPITAL

I turn 60 this summer so it was good to get checked out. The test was at Buchannan Hospital almost an hours drive from the prison and was my first time out of here in seven months. The car ride was great, I loved the feeling of being in motion and having the windows down and the wind blowing in. My Friend "Cuba" was the driver and we chatted a little, but mostly just enjoyed the ride.

The countryside was beautiful with the trees leafing out new yellow/green leaves and lots of spring flowers including lilacs and apples and some big patches of yellow mustard flowers. The air was perfumed with lilacs and honeysuckle. All this natural beauty in spite of how nasty this part of West Virginia is, lots of gas wells and the people in general keeping their places crowded with junk and debris, falling down buildings and broken down vehicles, and trashed out and cluttered yards in general. Still the drive was a real treat.

The upholstered chairs of the hospital waiting room and the hospital bed were so much more comfy than the plastic chair and steel bunk with a thin foam pad I've grown accustomed to. When a nurse apologized for my having to wait two-and-a-half hours in bed for the procedure to begin I told her it was no problem at all and as long as they didn't take more than three years we were all good. She laughed.

After the test they gave me lunch; a bowl of chicken soup, a sandwich, coffee, and apple juice. It was delicious. The simple truth is the best part of my mini sojourn was contact with women. Nothing to do with innuendo or sex, just some feminine company. Women are so different than men. Not better or worse. I know there are parts of humanity we share but there are distinctions too.

Rather than itemize the differences I'd suggest you imagine a world composed entirely of men. A world where women didn't exist. How would it differ from the world you know now? I'm surrounded constantly by 120-130 men 24 hours a day. They have their attributes and their detractions just as women do. But the genders are different from each other, Plus and Minus, Yin and Yang, magnetic polar opposites. I miss the company and compliment women bring to the world.

This is just one more aspect of prison life.

MAY, 2015

WILDFLOWERS

Early this morning, a bit before 6 am, I went down to the walking track. The sky was already growing light. I love how early the day begins with the solstice so near at hand. I walked the track twice, slowly. Most of this area is mowed regularly and kept short by the prison grounds crew. A few corners and culverts get to grow up a bit. I've been picking flowers here and pressing them in books. I consider the blooms before picking, appreciating their individual beauty as they are, where they are. I'm less concerned with their perfect conformity to type than I am with some immediate appeal factor I've yet to define. Sometimes beauty is quirky.

A few types of flowers, like a creeping legume ground cover, whose name I do not know, with small, brilliant yellow, snapdragon like blooms, press out better if I pick them in the cool, damp, dewy morning. Others work better if I wait until the late afternoon sun has dried them. Some, like Buttercups, close at night but are fully opened in the afternoon. Thick headed blooms like Red Clover and Daisies benefit from being drier before going into the book. Multi Flora Roses have little scent in the morning but by late afternoon are potently fragrant. I haven't figured out how to preserve the look of wild roses but when I open the book to the pages where they are pressing, the perfume is a powerful treat.

I carry a plain brown lunch bag to gather flowers in. I used to carry a paperback book, Shakespeare's Romeo and Juliet, and press the flowers as I picked them. This was cumbersome and very limited in the number of flowers it would hold. Also even though it is a love story, Romeo and Juliet is so tragic I thought it might subtly taint the emotion I was hoping to eventually impart in my arraignments. Instead a lunch bag allows me to bring back more flowers to my cube, uncrushed and unblemished.

I dump them onto a tissue, sort them by type, and trim off the undesired leaves, stems, and most of the unopened buds. This is the second time I get to scrutinize and contemplate the beauty of each bloom. In my tiny prison cubicle, amid the institutional grey/green of my surroundings I can slip into a world of yellow and white, purple and red, stamens, pistils and petals. The white and purple of the Creeping Vetch, the white and green of Dutch Clover, the leopard spots on pastel yellow of Autumn Olive, and the deep blue purple of Violets pleasing my eye and my aesthetic.

There are some flowers I enjoy but pass by, because they don't dry well for me. Two kinds of broad leafed Plantains, yellow Mustard and most varieties of Asters crumble or lose their petals when dry. Dandelions, if pollinated, turn to seed or, if not pollinated, brown as they dry.

The next step is to lay the blossoms in between the pages of my books. I pay close attention to detail choosing how each will lay and eventually present before crushing them from three dimensions into two. In a few days to a week I'll open the books and using tweezers transfer each flower to the pasteboards I save from the backs of my writing tables. There they air dry for a few hours on top of my locker. Then I put them back into a different, drier book to finish pressing and drying. This is the third time I can occupy my mind with their colors, complexity of design, and begin to consider the way I'll eventually lay them out.

Another week or two and they are ready. Mostly I make book markers, sometimes greeting cards. For pasteboard backers I prefer the separators that come in boxes of teabags from the commissary. Sometimes I cut out blank sections from used greeting cards. I lay out the primary flowers and glue them in place. Once the glue sets I lay out additional layers of flowers until I'm pleased with the result. Some have been as simple as a single Queen Anne's Lace, some have ten varieties . In every case I get to consider their beauty a fourth time, not only individually, but also how they relate to each other.

My favorite arrangements are from a perspective as if I were lying on the ground, viewing them horizontally. Sometimes I write a poem or Haiku, or sometimes I cut out text to accompany them. Most don't get any words. When the glue dries I laminate them with packaging tape I salvage from mail call. Tape is contraband here and owning a roll can get you in trouble. Laminated, they stand on the shelf above my desk space one or two or three at a time until I mail them out, or give them to other inmates to send to loved ones. This final display before mailing is the fifth time I get to enjoy them, arranged like flowery notes in a song about beauty in prison.

I've held for decades that we see what we look for. Though it's not always easy to remember, it is up to us to look around and perceive the world as either a prison or a garden.

PART 4. FOOD

When I was 20, I could walk forever. I was fit and strong and to spend the whole day walking was a pleasure. Kind of like the way riding in a car or truck is to me now that I am older and fat.

I could put my legs into auto drive and they would carry me anywhere. When I lived in the redwoods that was how I spent most of my days, walking in the hills, the canyons, and the beach. At times when I wanted human interaction I'd walk the three or four miles out to the highway and hitch hike to Jenner, or Gurneyville, or Sebastopol. A couple times I'd make the 100 plus miles trip to Berkeley. On summer Sundays there was a free concert in an apple orchard in Gurneyville. I don't recall exactly where but I went on a number of occasions and twice saw Ritchie Havens perform. It was all informal and relaxed and laid back.

It was Northern California in 1975 and that means something.

If you were there you know what it means. It was tie dye and bell bottoms and listening to acoustic music sitting in the grass in an apple orchard and everything was right. No one was famous and we were all celebrities

Afterwards, I'd swing by the Gurneyville food co-op when they were closed to check out their dumpster for goodies. Sometimes they'd leave the best stuff in a box on top. It was important to me to head back home before too late. It's almost impossible for a big guy to get rides after dark and I always felt safer to be in familiar woods after nightfall.

Somewhere along the way, someone showed me a plant called Miner's Lettuce. It grows on a short, succulent, almost translucent stem with a single round leaf the size of a quarter and is abundant in wet ground near springs and streams. They told me gold miners in the California gold rush era staved off starvation by eating it. I learned to eat a lot of it.

The groceries Ed brought me kept me fed about half the time. I did occasional odd jobs to make money and buy some food. I went hungry a lot, so the Miner's Lettuce came in handy.

In the summer after, a rain, giant puffball mushrooms would appear in the open grassland the sheep kept short. They'd get as big as large grapefruits and as long as they were pure white and firm they were good to eat. I only liked them cooked, preferably cut in thick slices and pan fried with some kind of oil and salt if I had it. Puff balls are bland at best but even bland foods can be improved by salt and hot oil.

There were many hundreds of acres of meadows scattered across the ridge tops, grazed by thousands of sheep and, when the weather was right I could find all the puffballs I could eat in a matter of minutes.

On a couple of occasions Ed visited over the weekend and would bring his rifle, a 30-30 lever action model 94 Winchester. I borrowed it and twice killed deer. The coastal range deer are tiny, perhaps 60 pounds live weight. Dressed out they might weigh 30 pounds and of this maybe 20 pounds of meat and liver was on a carcass.

I'd give a back leg to Ed and cook the rest, eating all of it in the next 3 days or so, starting with the liver.

Each day I'd recook it to keep it from spoiling. I spent a lot of time trying to kill a wild pig but they are much more elusive than the deer and I never got a shot at one. It was the exception when Ed brought his gun and he always took it home with him when he left. Out of nine months living in the redwoods I only had access to his gun about one week.

One thing I did notice walking around the ranch was the extraordinary number of sheep that died or were killed on the ranch. Two hired men on horseback, who I never met but often watched from my hidden places in the woods, would ride the hills to police the sheep and keep stray dogs in check. They rode with rifles in their scabbards tied to their saddles and shot quite a few stray dogs, which they'd often hang on the fences near the highway.

I guess it was supposed to be a message to other strays to keep out, but by reading the tracks on the ground it looked to me like it was no deterrent and served more as a point of interest that drew their attention. I could always find dead dogs or, more commonly, sheep, by watching the buzzards. Their circling in the sky made obvious the presence of carrion and, most days they found good work somewhere on the ranch.

The sheep were loosely tended, rounded up for shearing in the spring, though many were overlooked, and again in the fall when the lambs were sold for slaughter. The ones who escaped the spring roundup were encumbered by the weight of their fleece until it molted in summer. They refused to enter the deep woods and when I'd come to a meadow where they were grazing they'd bolt as a unit, the entire flock running away together. If I were anywhere in sight they'd run.

A common occurrence was to find dead lambs and I discovered from watching them that it was common for one of a set of twins to die and almost a guarantee that at least one from a set of triplets would succumb. At some point the running flocks brought out the wolf in me. Walking and running the ridges I could move the sheep across the hillsides, always staying above them as they in turn always stayed above the wood line. They preferred the higher ground but were too shy of me to come up so I could keep them moving across the steeper rougher ground.

I kept them in motion and eventually they would begin to tire. As they tired they slowed and in a single mad dash I ran down on to them, seizing a malingering ewe at the back of the stampede and tackling her. Once down she waited as sheep will do, and I was so surprised by my success that I wasn't sure of what to do next. I released her and she scurried back to her flock. I headed back to camp to think on it.

The next day I set to work and cut a stout oak staff about 4 feet long, 3 inches in diameter at the thick end and tapering to 2 inches at the narrow end. I peeled it and cut a slot 3 inches deep and as wide as the kerf of my bucksaw blade in the center of the narrow end. In my camp kit I had a bottle opener about five inches long and made of stamped steel. It was the kind with a round shape on one end for removing bottle caps and a triangular shape on the other end to punch holes in cans.

I hammered it flat and then worked it on a stone to sharpen both sides of the triangular end. I slipped it into the kerf cut in my staff where it fit snug but I knew it wouldn't stay there long. I took both shoelaces from my boots and cut one in half, using both halves to re-lace my boots. The other lace I used to bind the steel point in place transforming the staff into a spear. It took me a day to make. A long day, a thoughtful day, a hungry day.

When I work in my garden I like to think how much it connects me with my ancestors. People who, for the last 12,000 years, have grown their own food. People I don't know as individuals but with whom I'm deeply connected by our common experience. Likewise for the last 200,000 years people have spent hungry days sharpening sticks and thinking of the coming hunt. I spent that day with those people.

The next morning I climbed to the ridge top and searched for a flock of sheep. When I found them I worried them back and forth until some began to flag. Again the mad dash brought me along alongside a ewe with twin lambs. A quick jab brought down a lamb of about 40 pounds. It was down but not dead and I dispatched it with a quick blow to the head. I dragged it into the woods, skinned and gutted it, and buried the hide, head, feet and offal in a shallow grave in the woods. Pigs or dogs might dig it up but it would be hidden from the tell tale circling of the buzzards.

I carried the carcass and liver back to my camp, stopping en route at a spring to wash the blood from myself and the meat. That afternoon I built a fire and roasted the whole animal, gorging on the liver and haunches. During the next two days I finished it, maybe 12-15 pounds of meat in three days. Over the course of the next nine months I would run down, spear and kill another half dozen young sheep out of the thousands that lived on the range where I lived.

Later in life, I would own farm animals and I understand the down side of rustling livestock. I'm not advocating any such behavior here. I'm telling a story from my youth. I'm relating a time and a progression of events that I lived through. It is a story of a boy becoming a wolf, a story of learning to kill to eat, a story of a modern man in primal bloom.

There is a footnote to this story I want to add at this point. About four years later, not long after I met Diane, in the winter of 1978-1979, she and I would travel to California and spend the winter on this same piece of property. It's a great story in and of itself and I'll get to it at the right time for telling. By then Ed had built a house from a wine barrel and a big hydroponic greenhouse with a kitchen and spare room. Diane and I stayed three months in the greenhouse and in that time she got to explore all the places I've been writing about.

Together we've climbed into the hollow hearts of ancient redwoods and had many adventures together. But the footnote to this part of the story is that one evening we were lounging around and Ed told me he had something of mine. He went to get it and came back with my spear. Apparently he was enamored with it and had kept it over the intervening years. When he handed it to me I could feel a surge of energy from my youth in it, as if it were a powerful talisman. It was a reunion with an old friend of mine from a time of great hunting.

Ed offered to give it back to me but I decided to leave it with him. Last I heard he was living on Vancouver Island in British Columbia. I'll always be happy that Diane got to see these places and meet these people with me. Happy for the adventures we had together and having returned there with her helps me remember that this was not a dream.

FEBRUARY, 2015
LOCKDOWN

Four months down. The moon is almost full again. I like to use it like the side rail of a pool table making bank shots of love to my BabyO. Try it. It's a big moon, hard to miss. Just use your own BabyO.

I've not been keeping up on my letters or other writing. If I owe you a letter please be patient. All last week the adjacent Medium security prison has been on lockdown so our facility has been conscripted to provide manpower to cover for them. Lockdown is everyone confined to their cells 24 hours a day. This time it was for seven days, the longest since my stay, though some guys here remember lockdowns lasting up to 6 weeks.

According to the rumor mill, some amigos got into a dispute about which TV station to watch and a stab fest ensued. I remarked to a friend how trivial this seemed. He's been down lots longer than me and his response was that lots of guys up there are serving 20-40-60 years. Their lives are reduced to what fits in a locker. They have almost no self determination.

When you are left with crumbs of an ordinary existence they take on new proportions. Sometimes all you're left with is the choice between "Sabado Gigantica" and Spanish Edition "So You Think You Can Dance". Plus your self respect. When everything else is taken, whatever you are left with is the most important thing in the world.

Everyone in our facility is conscripted to work when a lockdown happens. No one is paid but if you don't work you earn a trip to the SHU (solitary housing unit, a nice name for the hole). Some guys do laundry. Each inmate has a net bag for dirty clothes with his name and cell/bunk number on it. The laundry worker dumps the clothes into a washer along with the bag. No sorting so even your whites turn a dirty brown/green. When the wash is finished it's thrown in a dryer, then back into the net bag and returned to their cell.

Five guys from here did the dirty laundry for 2,000 inmates up there. Other guys from here did snow removal/janitorial work in the common areas and in the guard's dining room and bathrooms. I worked on a crew making brown bag meals. Each bag contains two slices of fake cheese, two slices of baloney (B'low-me) loaf, four slices of bread or two hot dog buns, and two packs of fake Kool Aid with artificial sweetener so no one can make hooch out of it. Also they got oranges one time in seven days. More on that later.

We had a crew of 40-60 guys packing bags all day. We made 2,200 bags per meal, three meals per day. Yes they get the same bag for every meal. That's 6,600 meals a day for seven days. I mostly worked putting two slices of B'low-me loaf into plastic bags. This, like most prison food, is the lowest grade process meat legal for human consumption and looks like its made out of bruises and taints. It's the shit they won't put into pet food.

On a lighter note I did introduce the idea of folding a slice in half and using it as a meat puppet mouth. The idea caught on quickly and moved from barking and meowing to Motown harmonies, all being performed by B'Low-me loaf puppets. Sometimes you have to laugh to keep from crying.

I feel bad for the guys in lockdown. There may have only been 20 or 50 in the stab fest but all 2,000 get locked down. Three meals of B'low-me loaf a day and no showers. It must get pretty ripe up there. The laundry workers say it's disgusting. I heard a guy here who works on the garbage crew say that the first few days as many as a thousand bags were thrown away each meal. Eventually though, everyone runs out of their little food stashes and gets hungry.

By the end of the week they hauled away two busloads of offenders and life returned to normal. Sorry, that's actually a bunch of bullshit. Life here is anything but normal.

I mean to say life returned to crushing boredom, controlled movement, access to a shower, and 50 guys at a time crowded into a small room and trying to muscle their preference for watching "Sabado Gigantica" or Spanish edition "So You Think You Can Dance".

My friend Omar works nights here. He goes around to the powerhouse and waterworks every hour throughout the night and takes readings from the meters that measure power usage, water pressure, and gauges at the sewage plant. At the sewage plant all the incoming sewage passes through a large macerator that chews it up, much like a garbage disposal in a kitchen sink, except much bigger.

When the macerator gets overloaded it sidelines solids into a big bag that gets changed out and sealed up when it fills. Up the hill, during the middle of the lock down, inmates conspired to flush their oranges down the toilets all at once at midnight. The idea was to protest the lockdown by clogging the sewer system. Also, if the toilet were to back up into your cell you'd have to be moved to another cell while it was fixed and that at least would be something to do in an otherwise mind numbingly boring week. It's the same mentality as monkeys in zoos that bang their heads on the wall and throw poop at the tourists. It's something to do with what's at hand.

For better or worse the protest didn't work because all the toilets here are high pressure flushers with big sewage lines and all the oranges are very small. Almost all the fruit here is culls or undersized for commercial markets. The high power toilets are installed because clogging them up is one of the few ways inmates can find a voice that no one wants them to have. All the tiny oranges were effectively whisked out of the prison, just like the two bus loads of amigos. Down the hill 1,000 oranges flew, all the way to the sewage plant where they overwhelmed the macerator, were diverted to the solid waste bag, which exploded from their weight and spread them and other unmentionables everywhere. They were waiting for Omar at his 1 am meter reading. He spent most of the night cleaning the place up. That's what they pay him $26.00 a month for.

The moon will be up tonight, rising in the east an hour before sunset and setting before dawn in the west. If you find yourself outside, look for the moon, clear your head, consider the angle, and ricochet some love to your BabyO. If you find you have a little left over good will, maybe bank shot a bit of it to Omar. I'm sure he could use it.

JUNE, 2015
PRISON FOOD

The simplest way to think of the food here is in three categories:

First there are meals provided by the BOP. Breakfast is a very loose affair and only varies on a few holidays of the year. From 5-7 AM there is cold cereal, instant oatmeal or grits, and usually a partial case of fruit is set out. We get fruit once or twice a day. It's always culls or cosmetically defective or damaged, probably a good place for the purveyor to dump low quality produce. Sometimes it is bananas that have freezer burn, small or misshapen oranges or grapefruit, or apples that are dimpled, scabby, or turning brown in the core. When the fruit is good I try to stockpile several pieces. Guys that know I like it give me theirs, or sometimes I'll trade for something I have. There is usually skim milk and a hot chicory coffee substitute that tastes like cigarette ashes in hot water. Just serve yourself.

One or two inmates do the setup and breakdown of the breakfast bar. On holidays such as Thanksgiving, Christmas, Easter, and Memorial Day we have scrambled eggs and frozen waffles served as a hot breakfast. The trade-off is that on those days we have a sandwich in a bag for dinner. Sundays we have eggs and waffles for lunch. Usually there is also "Turkey Ham" a slab of homogeneous, rubbery meat composite dyed purple/red. In the past I've said that from the flavor and appearance I'd guess it is made from taints and bruises. This same ubiquitous processed material is extruded in several shapes and served as cold cuts, hot dogs, kielbasa, and sausage. It is generally despised and most often thrown away.

Lunch and dinner are interchangeable. Some kind of meat, a hot vegetable, and one, two, or three starches like white rice, noodles, pasta, tortilla wraps, or boiled potatoes. We have a salad about once a week. Think public school lunches and you know what we eat. There's plenty of food and it's easy to gain weight and lots of guys do. Quite a few inmates say the food is better here than at most BOP facilities. The quality sucks but there's plenty of it. Oils, fats, starches dominate.

The second kind of food is from the commissary. One day a week we can turn in a list of food to purchase at commissary. For us that's Tuesday morning. Everything is non-perishable so it can be kept in a locker.

There are a selection of snacks like crackers, chips, cookies, granola bars, chocolate, and tootsie pops. There are also proteins like peanut butter, tuna, sardines, Velveeta non perishable cheese food in a squeeze bottle, Slim Jims, and "summer sausage" which has an uncanny resemblance to "Turkey Ham". There are starches available , instant oatmeal, instant rice, instant potatoes, instant refried beans, ramen soup, and tortilla wraps.

Beverages include Tang (just in case we are planning on going to the moon), generic Kool Aid, hot chocolate, instant coffee and tea bags, plus lots and lots of Coca-Cola brand sodas.

Out of dozens of food choices there is one live food. For 55 cents I can, and do weekly, purchase 2 heads of fresh garlic. So do the guys I play cards with each evening and usually each evening we'll eat 3-4 cloves each. It's both healthy and humorous.

If you're wondering what's so funny about eating garlic, get together with 3 or 4 friends and each of you live in a closet in your house for a year or two. Every evening get together and eat some raw garlic before going back into your closet, and see if it doesn't make you laugh.

There are some points of commonality in the commissary offerings. Nothing is organic. Everything is prepackaged, prepared, and instant. Nothing requires refrigeration. It's all highly refined and contains too much sodium, along with oils like cottonseed, soybean, and palm, and is rich in aspartame. Except for the soda everything is packaged in plastic bags or pouches, no glass or metal cans.

Most of the popular items from the commissary are stockpiled by a couple of inmates who run "stores" where items can be purchased anytime at a significant markup. Because it's a cashless society items from the stores are paid for with postage stamps, the currency *du jour*, or by replacing it with the same thing, plus more, on commissary day.

As an example a pack of tuna which costs $1.60 at the commissary might sell for 5 stamps. Stamps sell for 49 cents each but are discounted to only have 40 cents purchasing value. There are also non food items available from the commissary such as toiletries and a few big ticket items like athletic shoes, MP3 players, and radios.

The third type of food is food prepared by inmates, using very limited ingredients from the commissary, saved from meals, and items that are "liberated" from the kitchen. Inmates prepare a remarkable diversity of tasty dishes, especially considering there are no cooking facilities.

There are a couple of opposing views on buying food from the kitchen. I don't do it because it's contraband and I don't want to do anything that might delay my getting home. I've seen too many guys lose years of good time and drug program incentives because of small things like tobacco or food.

One objection to the sale of food from the kitchen is that the food was originally meant for everyone, but I don't buy into that idea any more than do I buy the food itself. If a guy can make a couple bucks a week taking these chances, then good luck to him. Many men in the kitchen have been down 5, 10, 15, or even 20 years. In much less time than that, a man can become totally isolated from anyone on the outside.

It's a very rare individual who still receives financial support after a decade of incarceration. Men who make $16-20 a month have to live frugally and save a long time to buy $80.00 walking shoes. Doing without almost everything already, it's hard to cut back on 50 cents a day.

Wives move on with their lives, children become estranged, friends forget or move away or die. Warehoused people simply fade from view. Out of sight, out of mind. In spite of the lip service the BOP gives to the importance of maintaining family bonds, almost everything about the prison system destroys relationships between inmates and the world.

For the majority of the inmates doing serious time, the world devolves into a tiny cube, a bunk, and a locker. Add in a closed loop on a walking track and a bag of chips on Tuesday morning, and a real treat becomes a clandestine burrito made with instant refried beans, a part of a stolen tomato and some fake cheese for the Friday night card game.

Time for me to go. It's almost lunch.

CHANGES

What a moon last night and again this morning. Gigantic. Brilliant. At 5 AM the short grass was crystalline and appeared effervescent with reflected moon beams as I walked through it. The second full moon of winter turns January into February. We've reached a pivot point as days start earlier and night arrives later. Winter is not over but we've passed the hump of it and begun the slide to the new spring.

Kali Ma walks with the severed head of last year in her hand and wipes clean the slate for the next verse to be written.

All things are about to be made new. Our state of grace wriggles in its chrysalis. I can feel it coming. The snow and rain slake the ground to quench the coming summer. Tree roots stretch while the branches still rest. The last seed heads of foxtail grass finally bend and break and spill their seed on the ground that heaves with frost and covers them. In the sheltered sunny spots I've seen errant Dandelions stretching the parameters of the season, though as yet no pollinators to attend them.

I'm sure it won't be long now. The song that slumbered but never dies is awakening. The next verse is already writing itself. I can feel it coming.

THE PILL LINE

There are four or five nurses who work a rotation of shifts and tend to us at "Pill Line" each day, at 6 AM, and 2 PM. They disperse the medications that inmates are not trusted with such as narcotics, like painkillers, or drugs that can be weaponized, such as insulin. Twice each day, 30 or so inmates gather in the hall outside the nurses station to receive our due. Yesterday morning we waited until 7:30 in the morning before the nurse supervisor showed up. As she was unlocking the door she apologized for being late saying that several staff members had not shown up for work that day. Most of us didn't mind the wait. We weren't going anywhere. Personally, I always take a book, so while I waited I was on Safari with Hemingway in "The Green Hills of Africa".

By the afternoon a nurse had been called in on her day off, to fill in. She's a nice lady, though I can't recall her name. I've always been bad with remembering names. She's almost always pleasant and cordial. She, too, was an hour late and running ragged. When she unlocked the door to the nurses station she was obviously in a fluster. I was third in line. Ahead of me was "Mr. Smith" an inmate with a degenerative condition that has landed him in a wheelchair. All of the inmates collectively take care of the two inmates in wheelchairs. They are helped in every way, by everyone. This includes being advanced to the front of every line. That's a big deal in prison where line jumping is not tolerated.

Oddly enough, the door to the nurse's station is too narrow to allow Mr. Smith's wheelchair to pass through, so she has to bring his medication and cup of water out into the hall. This gets under her skin a bit. Also they have changed his medication without telling him. He is very polite and asks what the new pill is. She doesn't know. He asks what it does. She isn't sure. He is hesitant to take medication that neither he nor the nurse knows anything about. She is really getting put out now. By his lack of cooperation, by working on her day off, by being further delayed on a day when she is already running an hour late on her last chore before going home. She tells him to wait until she deals with everyone else in line and she will look it up in her book of pharmacology.

I'm next in line and I enter the nurse's station. I tell her my number, my name, and give her my ID card.

"Hello, how are you doing?" I ask.

"Not so good, today" she says. Usually she is very pleasant and good-natured. I try to cheer her up a bit.

"Is this your last stop today?" I ask, though I already know it's the case.

"Yes, it is." she says as she tears open the package my syringe is in. I pull my shirt out of my pants to expose a bit of my belly. She injects air into the bottle of insulin and extracts 20 units of solution.

"Has it been a tough day?" I ask.

"Yes, it has." she says. She hands me the syringe and I stick the needle into my belly.

"Well," I say "I'm sorry to hear that. I know it is small enough consolation, but I thank you for coming in to take care of us today." I put the used needle into the sharps disposal unit.

"It could be worse" I say.

"I don't see how" she says as she gives back my ID card I tuck my shirt back into my pants and pause a moment.

I lean toward her.

"I could be you. You could be me. I'm not going home today," I say to her quietly.

She is caught in time for just a moment. I see her go through some changes. I turn for the door.

"Thank you, Mr. Gariano" she says to me.

"Thank you again, for your service." I reply and leave.

I should really make it a point to learn her name.

JUNE, 2015

Today is the longest day of the year. I mean to say the day with the longest photoperiod, the longest stretch from sunrise to sunset. The solstice. The Earth is fully cocked and the northern biosphere is firing on all cylinders. The engine of life is roaring throughout the Appalachian mountains. Wildflowers either have bloomed, are blooming, or are getting ready to. Most of the trees have flowered and are maturing seeds, nuts, and acorns. The wild black raspberries are ripening just beyond the prison boundary. Life and Death and Life and Death and Life tumble together.

On the surrounding verdant hills are large swatches of dull brown in the forest canopy where the poplar trees are blighting en masse. On a few nearby ones I can see the leaves are crisping and curling, first at the tips, then progressively dying back toward the stems. There are a multitude of small spiky green caterpillars on them but I cannot tell if they are the cause of the dieback, or just taking advantage of the tree's weakened immune system.

No doubt there are bacteria and viruses at play along with parasitic and saprophytic fungi, all with a stake in the game. The caterpillars are occurring in such prolific numbers that they are attracting flocks of song birds to dinner. No doubt the birds are gorging and pooping and fertilizing the next generation of trees that will replace the poplar canopy and have their own day in the sun. The fierce and beautiful sun, which we will enjoy so much of today. Hail Ra in all his glory!

Yesterday we had fast moving storms with prolific lightning , thunder, and periods of driven, sheeting rain. Someone said it was the remnants of a hurricane that blew ashore in Texas a few days ago. By nightfall the ground here was saturated, though the prison grounds saturate quickly. The prison sits on a strip mine site and is covered in a thin layer of bright yellow clay subsoil that perks very slowly. Many new prisons (this one is eight years old) are built on environmentally toxic sites that are gifted to the BOP, who accepts them along with the complete transfer of all liability for any environmental hazards. This is a common practice for the extractive energy industry to escape responsibility and future liability.

Prisons are great places to hide crimes against nature. I'm reminded of the axiom about magic: The big motion hides the small motion. The big motion - see how we've sequestered the rule breakers that pose a threat to your safety, the small motion - toxic runoff seeps into and poisons the mountain stream, the tributaries, the rivers, the estuary, the bay, the gulf, the ocean.

By donating toxic land to public sector use (remember the public playground at Love Canal?) like the BOP, the mining company can avoid the cost of mitigating the ongoing environmental disaster and get a tax write off for the inflated valuation of the land. This insures that a greater margin of profit is preserved for both the mining concerns and the prison system. Fuck everyone else downstream.

At first glance it appears the bad guys have beat the system, that they've subverted if not aborted the natural order. Not to worry. Nothing prevents the wheel from turning. Nobody gets out alive.

The prison also serves the fossil fuel industry by consuming vast quantities of energy. Prisons have enormous carbon footprints and transfer gigantic sums of tax dollars to the energy conglomerates. They are overt consumers of petrochemicals and fuels, natural gas, and coal.

Much of this consumption is in the form of electricity. The fences and lights burn 24/7/365. Tall light towers with banks of high pressure sodium lights illuminate this mountain hollow from dusk until dawn. In the evenings I watch the martins and bats glide and dip and swoop to eat the innumerable insects from the dark forest that surrounds us.

Is there anything as beautifully athletic as a martin in flight? They come to eat the insects that are drawn to the lights that burn the electricity created by generators devouring the coal stripped from the mountain sites of tomorrow's prisons.

Everything is a wheel and I am both a spoke in the wheel and a witness to the circumambulation.

I was playing cards last night when Black Mike came and got me. "Can you come with me?" he asked. "It's important. I have to show you something."

We headed outside, around the corner of the building. Near the back, under the brilliant glare of a security light was an extraordinary moth. Bigger than a Luna moth, with a wingspan wider than my hand is long, it clung to the concrete wall. It fanned it's wings very slowly and occasionally had full body tremors. It seemed on the crux of life, and I couldn't tell if it was dying or had just been born.

Exclusive of the wings, it's body was the size of the last two joints of my little finger and bright red and white. I picked it up by the wings and it offered no resistance. I moved it higher on the wall where it clung again, but did not fly. I put it in my Tupperware bowl and snapped on the lid. Inside the housing unit I showed it to many of the guys who live here, to a chorus of oooohs and aaaahs! A beautiful, sacred fairy of the woodland come to visit us in the shithole.

Later that night my friend Chicken came to get me because another moth of the same type was beating itself against a lit window. When I got there it was lying stunned on the window sill. I collected it in an empty peanut butter jar. By morning, before first light, the second moth was dead. The first moth seemed in fine shape and before dawn I carried it far from the lights of the housing unit, back to the edge of the woods. I gently spilled it out beneath a raspberry briar. Now four hours later it has climbed high on a thorny stem.

The Blue Jays that come to pick berries are eyeing it up, but I'm sitting, writing, 10 feet away. They are ineffectual at yelling me away. Maybe the moth will fly off, lay eggs, and die. Maybe some of the eggs will grow to be caterpillars that will eat the poplar trees. Maybe some of the caterpillars will be eaten by birds while others will morph into beautiful moths emerging next summer on the eve of the solstice. Maybe some of the moths will be drawn to the lights to die in prison. Or maybe the Blue Jay will eat it as soon as I leave.

Tremendously important to the moth and Blue Jay, a matter of life and death, it doesn't matter much to me. Just like them I am a spoke in the wheel, and a witness to it's turning. The wheel driven by Ra, on this, the longest day of the year.

MORE ON COOKING

No we don't have a microwave. They said it won't be coming back. The reason I heard is that at some facilities inmates have used them to heat oil or water and thrown it onto other inmates faces as they slept. It's an anonymous way to attack someone. One guy here had his face scalded with water this way and was moved here as a protective measure. I can't tell if this is why, for real, or if it's one more way for the guards to mess with us.

Here's how everything is cooked. One water fountain dispenses hot water at 190 degrees for making coffee and cup o soup type products.

Guys also use it for things like instant mashed potatoes and quick rice. It also works for Ramen noodles. Other things like quesadillas or soft tacos are wrapped in a plastic bag (everything is cooked in and eaten out of plastic), then tied shut and put in a bowl lined with another bag. The second bag is filled with hot water, the air pushed out of the bigger bag, then tied shut. The lid snapped onto the bowl, and the whole thing wrapped in a towel . Let it sit for 10-20 minutes, changing the hot water once or twice depending on what and how much you're cooking. Viola!

Sardines, mackerel and tuna all come in plastic pouches because we are not to be trusted with cans or anything that could open them. They can be preheated by submerging them in hot water before opening. Here's a classic recipe: Submerge and preheat a bag of mackerel, then punch holes in it with a dedicated ink pen (otherwise your letters smell like fish) and squeeze out all the liquid into a toilet. Flush, then pour the contents into a bowl. Add mashed potato powder and hot water according to directions. Add stolen onions and green peppers, if you have a kitchen connection, diced small, if you have something to cut them with. Stir everything, snap on the lid, wrap in a preferably clean bath towel and wait until it stinks like a commercial fisherman's boots. Unwrap and open. If it looks like cat diarrhea it's done. Serves one or two people so sick of institutional food that this seems appealing.

How about garbage can ice cream? Wash out the little garbage can you share with the other guy you bunk with. Fill with ice and leave room for the same bowl you cooked your mackerel in . pour in milk you put in a water bottle and stuffed down your pants from the lunch line. Stir in as many little individual serving packs of jelly as you can get. If you don't have enough jelly you can add a few packs of artificially sweetened fake Kool-Aid. stir occasionally until it forms a runny custard texture and pretend it's ice cream and doesn't taste like mackerel.

APRIL, 2015

FOUR-LEAF CLOVERS

I've been reading quite a bit lately and there are several books that I keep revisiting. Some ideas take a bit to soak in. One such book has been James Gleik's "Chaos" that describes the nature of creation (including biological), variation, and selection. It does a terrific job of explaining the idea of fractals and the graphic depictions of them explain, without words, much of the nature of the physical world. I've been thinking of this quite a bit lately and it came to mind again this morning while I was writing a letter to my friend of 40 years and I thought I'd forward an excerpt from my letter as a greeting to everyone this morning. Happy Spring.

"It has been wonderful seeing spring arrive. I get to spend most of the days outside and watching the seasonal progression always pleases me. Dandelions are blooming like crazy, the colt's foot has already gone to seed, at the edge of the woods the redbud is blazing and the green-gray-white of the dogwood blooms began to show yesterday. I've heard turkeys calling for the past few weeks and I've seen numerous bright orange salamanders. One of my favorite heralds of spring has been the chorus of peeper tree frogs on warm evenings and mornings.

A funny thing this week was that a friend of mine, Chicken F., pointed out a four leaf clover (white dutch) as we were walking on the walking track here. The walking track is a circular path around a combination football/softball field, about 1/4 mile long, with grasses, weeds and clover on either side. When I commented that I'd only seen a few in my life he told me he finds them "all the time". Of course "all the time" is a relative statement. Then he began to show me. Over the next few days, in a total of about 5 hours of searching, he found more than 60 four leaf clovers, while I found a half dozen.

He says it's always the same with white dutch clover. He has an "eye" for them, finding them in clumps I've just searched methodically without any luck. The standard joke is, "how lucky can a four leaf clover be if you pick it in prison?" Still, I find it entertaining to look for them, press them, laminate them in tape. In many ways the variations in leaf patterns (we've found several with 5 leaves and 1 with 6) speaks directly to chaos theory, that the constant variations in biological entities both provide opportunities for change (natural selection) and the extremes/variations actually define the center instead of disproving it.

The norm is not only defined by its constancy in reproduction but in its diminishing frequency of variations from the standard. The exception does prove the rule. All life, including our own lives, are part of an extraordinary wheel, and some of the pleasure is found in the occasional wobble in the turning.

Celebrate who you are where you are. Life is long and full of mystery. The wheel of life inexorably carries us home, the wobbles are just variations in the route.

MAY, 2015
QUIET TIME
It is the middle of the second half of the night, about 3:30 am. I've been awake for more than an hour. This is the quietest time in prison. I cannot hear anyone talking.

How rare this is.

There is plenty of snoring, and the air exchangers of the ventilating system produce a low level background roar. Every few minutes a toilet flushes. In a room where 130 men sleep, the toilets never do. There is enough light for writing at my desk even though this is technically the "lights out" period from 9:30 pm to 5:30 am. Lights out in prison means every other one of the overhead fluorescent lights are turned off. In a modern prison it is never dark. To darken the head of our bunk for sleeping we hang up a towel or shirt or folded blanket on the end of our bed. We call it a tent. Sometimes a guard in a pissy mood will yank down all the tents in the middle of the night, and throw them on the floor, daring anyone to complain. This happens several times a month.

Every minute or two someone goes past where I'm sitting in the shuffling gait of a man in flip-flop shower shoes, who has to pee but wishes he were asleep. Then a toilet flushes and a moment later he shuffles by in the opposite direction. I've had a week or two of waking up for a few hours in the middle of the night. Usually I lay quietly so as not to disturb the man sleeping in the bunk 18" above me, and I think. Mostly of the people I know. Is my family well fed, well loved, healthy? Are my friends doing okay? Are people coping well? I can't affect their circumstance from where I am. That's a new development for me. On the outside I'm a problem solver. In here, not so much.

Now it's 4:30. I write slow. The toilets keep flushing through the night like some erratic aquatic timepiece. In 30 minutes two guards will walk past, spaced 50 feet apart, each with their keys jingling. They are counting us. They do it every two hours all night long, every night. The jingling of their keys as they walk by is another timepiece of sorts, every two hours on the nose. What a shit job.

I've been reading "On Writing" by Stephen King. He says the most fundamental requirement for a writer is a place to write in where he can shut the door and close out the world. That is never going to happen here in the monkey cage. Maybe this quiet in the middle of the night will be as close as I can get. The pace of the toilet flushing is picking up. Some of the guys here have jobs and are getting up for work. Still nobody is talking. It's so nice.

In the daytime the clamor and din are enough to whack you the fuck out, if you let it get under your skin. But for now it's relatively quiet, just some shuffling, some toilets flushing, some guys hacking up phlegm and blowing their noses in the sink, quite a bit of snoring and in a couple of minutes the jingling keys of my kidnappers. In the still of the night.

I'd better go pee.

PART 5. DALE

This last week my friend, I'll call him Dale, has been living out one of the greatest fears for a family man in prison. It's had a profound effect on many of us who know him. He's in his 50's and has been down for 30 plus months with what remains of a 121 moth sentence to go. He was convicted of possession of 50 grams of meth which he told me was his personal stash.

At the time of his arrest he'd been smoking meth for about 5 months. He was married and his wife was a heavy drinker. They'd thought she was unable to conceive until she did. Their baby was born with severe fetal alcohol syndrome and required significant therapy to which she was responding well. He never blamed his wife, seeing that she struggled with her own demons.

By the time his daughter was 2 years old, methamphetamines provided Dale with the energy to work 60 hours a week, and care for his daughter and wife.

He has a big heart and he was spending it on taking care of everyone but himself. One day, exhausted, he fell asleep in his car with the meth in his glove compartment. He was awakened from his nap by a cop tapping on his window and in the next few minutes his world turned to shit. He was a good father, a good husband, and a good man with a bad habit.

In many modern countries he would have been ordered to addiction treatment and been able to continue to care for his family and make a living. Countries that are smarter and kinder than America and countries in which the prison industry doesn't have such a throttle hold on the politicians and public. Dale's case caught him 121 months in federal prison, Dale's daughter was sent to foster care in her aunt's custody, and Dale's wife was left alone to fend for herself with an addiction to alcohol that she could not control and no baby or husband.

The alcohol that plagued her is available in every convenience store, grocery, or neighborhood bar as long as you're willing to pay the state and federal governments a tax on every drink. Highly addictive, no known medicinal use, and a lethal intoxicant, alcohol meets every requirement of a schedule one drug but is legal in every state, advertised in every media, and provides a revenue stream for corporations and governments who in turn subsidize and promote it's use.

It is directly responsible for hundreds of thousands of deaths and destroyed lives each year in America. Alcohol is condoned by law, encouraged by business, and romanticized by advertising. This story is one Madison Avenue will never tell

During the last almost three years of Dale's incarceration his wife has continued to drink. Earlier this year she began to suffer from liver and kidney failure, a direct result of her alcohol consumption. She was hospitalized and received Dialysis treatments but even so her body continued to wither.

On Thursday last week she was sent to Hospice in Bristol, Tennessee. Dale applied to the BOP for a 10 hour furlough to go see his wife and daughter together one last time. A four hour drive there, two hours to visit , and a four hour return trip. The BOP rejected his request.

He is a nonviolent drug offender convicted of a victimless crime and the BOP would not give him 10 hours out of his more than 10 year sentence to say goodbye, to tell her he loves her, to hold his daughter while her mother dies. 10 hours. Can't do it. Impossible.

Friday morning as the sun came up Dale and I sat outside and he told me his stories. He's short and wiry and covered in tats. On the outside he rides a Harley.

On better days he's hilariously funny and fun to hang out with. He told me how much he loved his wife and how much he loves his daughter. He told me how difficult it was to find the energy and the hours in the day to make an honest living and care for his family. He told me how the meth made it all possible for at least a short time. He told me how it all came crashing down.

We stayed outside, him talking, me listening, until 8:30 or so then we went back in the housing unit.

About 10 am he walked up to me and told me he'd just received an email saying that his wife had passed away that morning.

She died alone in Hospice while we sat outside under the lightening sky, the sodium lights, and the all seeing eye.

She died while we sat there quietly and he professed his love for her.

I gave him a brief hug, he sobbed a few times, then went back to his bunk to be as alone as you can in a room of 130 men. The few convicts who saw us averted their eyes, sensing something was wrong, already having their own shit to deal with.

Sometimes the best thing you can give a guy in here is to look away for a few minutes.

An hour later Dale went to the counselors station to request a 10 hour furlough to attend his wife's funeral. His request was denied again.

Again the BOP could not spare him for 10 hours of his 10 year sentence to allow him two hours to sit by his deceased wife and hold his daughter. Can't do it. Impossible.

The constant heartache and biggest fear of every family man in prison is that we are not where we are needed. We cannot attend to the people we love. We fear that our absence will create a void that our families and the people we love will stumble into when we are not there to protect them.

There are many degrees of loss. Prison is crowded and loud. It's rarely quiet and almost never private. This is a great loss for me. Not the greatest, but for me the loss of privacy and the noise is significant. However the world is a perfect mirror and as such is filled with dichotomies. The constant closeness of other people presents its own opportunities to witness the human condition.

Monday morning. This morning I was outside by 5am. It was extraordinarily warm, the warmest morning of the year so far, with a heavy damp breeze blowing steadily. The sky here marches West to East most days and was again this morning. The clouds were thickly clotted and created a low ceiling of matted curds. There were a very few breaks through which I could see a less than half of the moon directly overhead.

The cloud cover broke apart as the sun came up. The heavy moisture in the air refracted the horizontal light into scarlet and crimson. The lighter the day grew the more the clouds broke apart. With the sun just above the horizon the sky was a mixture of cloud islands coursing through an azure sea. How I love the mornings.

I'm sitting at a table outside in the prison yard. It is a table made of rubber coated, heavy steel mesh with four steel seats welded to it. Thirty feet behind me a 25 foot tall wooden pole and mounted to the top of it is an all seeing eye, a remote controlled camera that swivels and zooms or fades, controlled by a guard who watches me through his monitor as I watch the sky. We both see what we look for.

SHRIMP BOATS

The first time I worked at sea I was just a boy, 18 years old. That time I spent three-quarters of a year on shrimp trawlers in the Gulf of Mexico, out of Galveston, Texas. I left Texas after that run and adventured around for a couple years, eventually returning for another stint of shrimping just as the rest of the country was preparing for winter. The southeast coast of Texas was a good place to winter in the mid 1970s. Friends I'd made in Galveston during my first foray on the water still owned the fish and ice house at the 6th Street docks.

While I was looking to crew on a boat they gave me hourly wage work on some of their fleet, while the boats were in dock. This allowed me to connect with captains and riggers looking for crews and to make a few bucks in the meanwhile. It was mostly hot, hard, and dirty work. Jobs like painting the outriggers with rust inhibiting black enamel and scrubbing out the engine rooms and bilges where diesel fuel that leaked from the big Caterpillar engines accumulated and mixed with the seawater that leaked in around the through hull fittings on the propeller shafts.

They also let me sleep on the boats I was working on. It was an equitable arraignment. I was a good worker and they had an infinite amount of grunt work that needed to be done. Over the next 7 or 8 months I'd come back to work there several times when I was between fishing trips.

The boats I crewed on were 45-70 feet long, both steel and wood hull, and carried crews of 3-6 hands. The best boats to work on were the ones where the captain was the owner or a part owner. Boats that were owned by investors or that were part of a fleet had captains that were employees. These boats were more of a crap shoot when it came to catching shrimp. Catching shrimp meant making money.

Winter turned to spring and spring turned to summer. Late that summer I was back working at the 6th Street docks when I was approached by a guy looking to outfit a boat docked in Port Bolivar, just across the channel from Galveston. He was middle aged, a hard and rough man as many men who work on the water are. He was short and thick with muscle. He captained for an owner who's health no longer permitted him to shrimp. He introduced himself as "the Finn". In all the time I knew him I never learned his real name. In retrospect I wonder if he had one.

We spent a week getting the boat, a 55-foot steel hull trawler, in shape for a trip. The whole of the week the Finn kept reassuring me he'd hire another hand or two to help out, but help never materialized. During that week, on two different occasions, the Finn intimated that he could connect me with friends of his that could "use someone like me." I guess the appeal here is to someone who enjoys being used. I'm not one of those people.

One scheme involved smuggling drugs, he said, from Cuba. The other was working as a mercenary in Africa. I assumed he was talking in hyperbole to inflate his image in my eyes, and that he made these macho allusions to sound tough and connected to tough guys.

It was impossible to discern with this guy what was real and what was imagined on his behalf. I never encouraged him along these lines. Instead I worked hard to get the boat ready and he promised me a generous share when we finally got around to catching shrimp.

The day before we were scheduled to head out we filled the hold with crushed ice, the fuel tanks with diesel, and bought enough groceries to feed four guys for two weeks. The Finn assured me that he'd have 2 more hands on the boat by first light, in time to head out with us. That evening I made us dinner, cleaned the galley, and headed to bed. The Finn headed out to the bars. Later that night, around closing time, I was awakened by the Finn and two other guys. All three were drunk as skunks as they stumbled and careened their way onto the boat.

They were loud and still drinking heavily from bottles of liquor they carried with them. They took seats in the galley and I got up to make a meal and coffee. It was 2 or 3 in the morning. We were supposed to leave around 6. As is often the case with drunks all three were filled with bravado, cajoling each other with one-upsmanship tales of daring do.

Their conversation took a dark turn with the Finn, daring the others and myself into taking (read stealing) the boat to some backwater chop shop he knew of in Louisiana. There we could get what he called Big Money for it. No doubt. Even at that time the boat and all its equipment was probably worth a couple hundred grand and he probably thought of Big Money as ten thousand dollars. All three of these guys carried handguns which had made their way out onto the table. I interjected several times that this was all crazy talk and that we were scheduled to go fishing in just a few hours, but my opinion was dismissed.

They soon badgered each other into a commitment to steal the boat. As the most sober one, I was sent below to start the engine. This involved starting a smaller gasoline engine the size of a pick up truck motor, called the power plant. The power plant was used to keep our batteries charged and to provide the initial torque to turn over the big Caterpillar diesel engine that drove the propeller. I went to my bunk, threw my gear into my bag. I went down the ladder from the galley, through the engine room, and up another ladder onto the back deck. I got off the boat and started walking toward the coast guard sub-station near the breakwater that protected the mouth of the channel. Behind me I heard the engine come to life on the boat and the boat pulling out of the dock, banging into other boats tied alongside, and making its way to the channel.

I could see they were running in darkness with no lights on. The sub-station was manned by two boys my own age that called in the theft to their superiors, who then decided that nothing was to be done before morning light. I waited at the substation until morning when the police came and got a statement from me. They gave me a ride back to the 6th Street docks in Galveston where the theft was the hot gossip topic for the day. I stayed on boats belonging to the fish house the next couple of nights.

Two days later the boat was found run aground on the beach somewhere near Louisiana. The bedding had been dragged to the engine room and doused with diesel fuel. A fire had been set but burned out before much damage was done. Along with the bedding were the bodies of the Finn's two drinking buddies, both shot and killed execution style. The Finn was nowhere to be found. The following morning I gave another statement to the police, basically reaffirming my initial statement. The next day I left Texas.

I got off that boat roughly 40 years ago. Sometimes when we are standing at the crossroads of our life it's hard to imagine the ramifications of the decisions we are making.

In retrospect, I wouldn't trade those years for anything, even if I could.

In my prison housing unit there is a bulletin board and sometimes someone will post an inspirational message. On it right now is an unattributed quote.

It says "I never met a strong person with an easy past". Ain't that the truth.

EPILOGUE

Greetings Friends,

Now June rolls into July. In prison guys like to say "One more day/week/month closer to going home". I have mixed emotions about this way of looking at time passing. Having just turned 61 I think of each passing day as also one day closer to dying too. Not to sound morbid or depressing but I consider my mortality daily, however ill defined my final day is.

If I see my life as a timeline with a finite starting point, my birth, and an indefinite ending, my death, there's no logical way to see myself distancing from one end of this spectrum without getting closer to the other end. Again, I don't find this perspective depressing. Instead I use it to initiate getting my joy out of each day, wherever I am. I can't just live for the future. I need to engage and enjoy the here and now.

My incarceration is a condition of my life that I cannot control. My cognitive process is still up to me though, and the consequences that follow will flow directly from my thoughts. This is the path that led me here and it will in large part determine my future. The joy I live with or without each day is a direct result of my attitudes and actions right now.

Years ago someone taught me that our lives are analogous to fruit. We are never static, we are always ripening or rotting. So I cannot waste these days in prison by just discarding them as quickly as possible. I need to relish each one and have some joy while I can, where I can.

This morning I spent an hour tutoring another inmate and began writing this. The entire time he has been working on a 2 page paper on what he hopes to get out of the Residential Drug Program. In an hour

78

he wrote half of one page. It's an arduous process. He and I work for an hour each morning starting after cell inspections at 7:30 am and we go until 8:45 when he goes to G.E.D. class. He does all his own writing and formulating sentences. Mostly I help with spelling and grammar. He has a significant speech impediment so sounding out the words often doesn't work for him.

Working together five days a week for the past couple months, I see great progress. We both delight in his improvements. He has been down for more than 12 years with just over two more to go. He is 47 and married and has three kids in their late teens. He's serving a 240 month sentence for selling crack cocaine. Last year he got some time off because of an across the board sentence reduction for crack cocaine cases. He'll get a couple years off for good behavior and a year off for the drug program. All told he'll still serve about 15 years total. Serving that much time is impossible to imagine. Having already served 12 years without being able to read or write is even harder to grasp.

Reading is such a refuge for so many inmates. Teaching a grown man to read is something I'd never taken the time for out in the world and I had no idea how rewarding it could be. Thinking less about myself and focusing my attention on someone else's plight, a total stranger, has been an unexpected pleasure. It's a great way to bring joy into both of our lives.

So, not to pontificate, but my unsolicited advice is if you feel like your life needs more joy, if you feel like time is slipping through your fingers, if you feel like you are a victim of your circumstance, try reaching out. Try being a part of the tide that raises all boats.

Remember that good or bad, you can give nothing away. The world is a perfect mirror. Shine into it.

Big Love,
Dave, 29655-057

ACKNOWLEDGMENTS

My thanks and Big Love go to my friend and editor David Straughan who encouraged me and did all the editing and arranging, as well as bringing this book to publication.

I owe an enormous debt of gratitude to Richard Hendel for the help with, among other things, the design of this book. I would also like to thank Dr. Dulcie Murdock Straughan for all of the help and guidance with putting on its finishing touches.

My indebtedness goes to my wife Diane Hall, the love of my life, who has given me love, family, encouragement, forgiveness, help, and a purpose in life. I owe her everything that is good in my life.

She pushed me to write, kept me connected, and has stood by me through thick and thin for 40 years.

ARTIFACTS

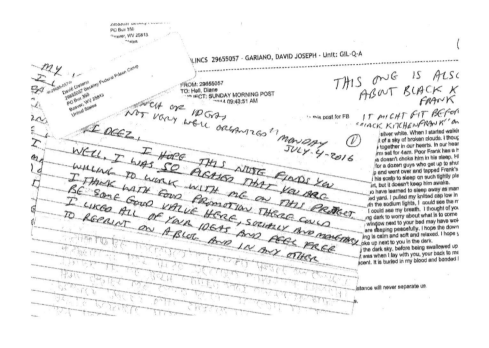

correspondence and beginnings of Big Love, 29655-057

85

Dave and Diane, 2013

Dave and Diane, 2016

In Memoriam card, Frank "Black Kitchen Frank" Jordan

Bracelet made by Frank for Diane

flower pressings made by Dave at Beckley

self-portrait by Dave at Beckley

"If the sight of the blue skies fills you with joy, if a blade of grass springing up in the fields has power to move you, if the simple things of nature have a message that you understand, rejoice, for your soul is alive."

- Eleonora Duse

Made in the USA
Middletown, DE
15 April 2018